CONTEMPORARY

ADVANCED

reading
basics

A REAL-WORLD APPROACH TO LITERACY

 **Education**

Bothell, WA • Chicago, IL • Columbus, OH • New York, NY

Image Credits: **Cover** Lisa Fukshansky/The McGraw-Hill Companies

www.mheonline.com

Send all inquiries to:
Contemporary/McGraw-Hill
130 East Randolph Street, Suite 400
Chicago, IL 60601

ISBN: 978-0-07-659099-5
MHID: 0-07-659099-2

Printed in the United States of America.

6 7 8 9 10 11 QVS 21 20 19 18 17

Contents

To the Student

Reading Basics will help you become a better reader. Research in evidence-based reading instruction (EBRI) has shown that reading has four important components, or parts: comprehension, alphabetics, vocabulary, and fluency. *Reading Basics* provides evidence-based reading instruction and practice in all four components. With your teacher's help, you can use the *Student Edition* and the articles in the *Advanced Reader* to gain important skills.

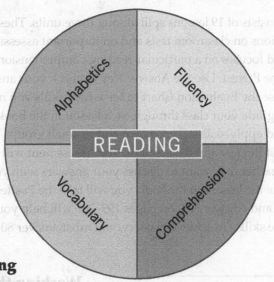

The Four Components of Reading

Comprehension *Reading Basics* teaches you many ways to improve your reading comprehension. Each lesson in the *Student Edition* introduces a different reading comprehension skill. You apply the skill to passages and to a workplace document. You also apply the skill to the articles in the *Reader*. Your teacher will help you use monitoring and fix-up reading strategies. You will learn ways to clarify your understanding of passages that are confusing to you. In addition, each article in the *Reader* begins with a before-reading strategy. At the end of the article, you will complete comprehension and critical thinking exercises.

Alphabetics In the *Student Edition* lessons, you will learn and practice alphabetics. Alphabetics includes phonics and word analysis skillls, such as identifying syllable patterns and accented syllables, correctly spelling plurals and homophones, and studying word parts, such as prefixes, suffixes, base words, and roots. You can use alphabetics skills to help you read and understand difficult words. For more practice, go to www.mhereadingbasics.com and use *PassKey*. This online program provides skills instruction and guided feedback.

Vocabulary Studying academic vocabulary will help you as a learner. Your teacher will present and explain five academic vocabulary words that you will need to understand as you read each *Student Edition* lesson. You will have a chance to practice these words along with other important vocabulary skills such as recognizing and using synonyms, antonyms, and context clues.

Your teacher will also present and explain vocabulary words important to your understanding of the articles in the *Reader*. As you read each article, notice that some words are defined in the margins. Use the definition and the context of each word to help you understand it.

Fluency Your teacher will present activities to help you with fluency—that is, reading smoothly, quickly, and accurately. You will practice fluency with the passages in the *Student Edition* and the articles in the *Reader*. You can also go to www.mhereadingbasics.com to download MP3 recordings of the articles. Listening to fluent reading will help you develop your own fluency skills.

How to Use This Book

The *Student Edition* consists of 19 lessons split among three units. These lessons help prepare you for questions on classroom tests and on important assessments. Each lesson is eight pages long and focuses on a particular reading comprehension skill.

Begin by taking the Pretest. Use the Answer Key to check your answers. Circle any wrong answers and use the Evaluation Chart to see which skills you need to practice.

Your teacher will guide your class through each lesson in the book. You will have chances to practice and apply skills on your own and in small groups. At the end of each unit, complete the Unit Review and Assessment. The Assessment will help you check your progress. Your teacher may want to discuss your answers with you.

After you complete the lessons in the book, you will take the Posttest on pages 189–198. The Evaluation Chart and Answer Key on pages 199–200 will help you see how well you have mastered the skills. To achieve mastery, you must answer 80 percent of the questions correctly.

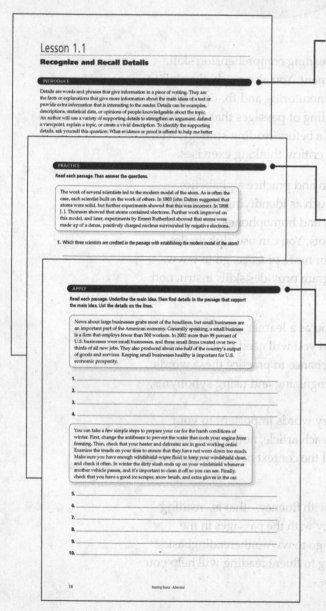

Working through Each Lesson

Introduce The first page of each lesson presents the reading skill. It also includes an example. Your teacher will use this example to explain and model the skill. Then your teacher will work with your class to do the guided practice at the bottom of the page. You will have a chance to practice this skill in the activities. Later in the lesson you will apply this skill to a document similar to one that you might use in the workplace.

Practice Next comes a page for practice. Usually, you will read a passage and answer questions about it that relate to the reading skill. You may be asked to fill out a graphic organizer to respond to a question. On some pages, there will be several passages followed by questions.

Apply The Apply page gives you a chance to apply the reading skill in a different way. In many lessons, you will read a passage and answer questions about it. You will see a variety of formats, including open-ended questions and graphic organizers.

Check Up The last page in the reading skills section of the lesson is the Check Up page. The questions on this page are always presented in a multiple-choice format. The Check Up page allows your teacher to monitor your progress as you learn the reading skill. Then your teacher can help you if you still have questions about the skill.

Workplace Skill The Workplace Skill page gives you another chance to practice the reading skill. Instead of using a reading passage, this page introduces the types of documents that you might find or need to use in the workplace. There could be a memo, a section of a handbook, or some kind of graph. You will read or study the document and answer questions about it.

The Workplace Skill documents relate to a wide variety of jobs. Some may be familiar to you, while others may be new.

Write for Work A Write for Work activity is at the top of the next page. You will do workplace-related writing such as drafting a cover letter or a set of procedures. The writing relates to the document on the Workplace Skill page. This activity provides a chance for you to practice your writing skills and reading comprehension at the same time.

Reading Extension In most lessons, a Reading Extension comes next. Here you apply the reading skill to an article in the *Reader*. After reading the article, you will answer multiple-choice and open-ended questions.

Workplace Extension Some lessons have a Workplace Extension instead of a Reading Extension. The Workplace Extension addresses work-related issues. These might include dealing with an overtime request or negotiating for a raise. You will read a scenario in which a person is faced with a work problem or issue. Then you will answer questions about how the person handled the situation or what he or she should do next.

For each unit, your teacher will hand out a Workplace Skill Activity sheet. You will work with a partner or in small groups to practice skills similar to those in the Workplace Extension. Many of these activities include role-playing so that you can practice realistic conversations about the workplace.

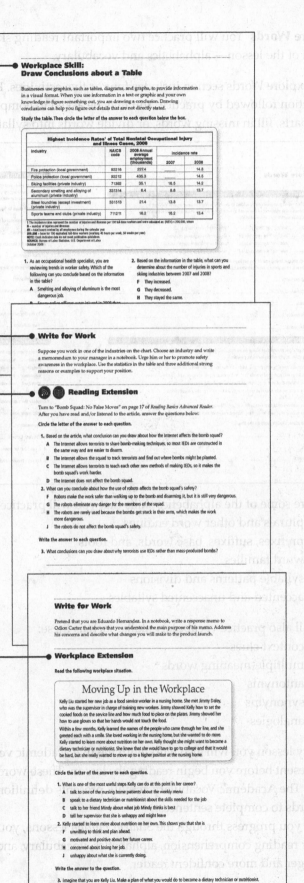

Explore Words You will practice two important reading skills in the Explore Words section of the lesson— alphabetics and vocabulary.

Each Explore Words section includes four or five activities. Each activity begins with brief instruction followed by practice. You may be asked to complete matching exercises, circle word parts, fill in missing words, or divide words into syllables.

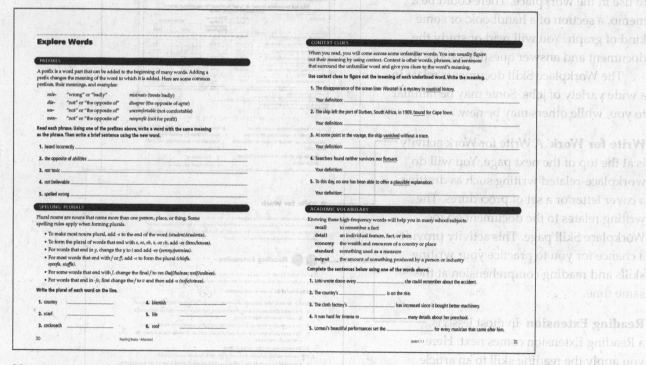

Here are some of the alphabetics skills that you will practice:

- plurals and other word endings
- prefixes, suffixes, base words, and roots
- word families
- syllable patterns and divisions
- accented and unaccented syllables

You will also practice vocabulary skills, such as these:

- context clues
- multiple-meaning words
- antonyms
- synonyms
- analogies

In every lesson you will also work with the five academic vocabulary words your teacher will present before you begin reading the lesson. These words appear in context in the lesson. The Academic Vocabulary activity presents definitions of the words. You will use the words to complete sentences.

As you progress through the *Student Edition* lessons, you will notice improvements in your reading comprehension, alphabetics, vocabulary, and fluency skills. You will be a stronger and more confident reader.

Pretest

Read each passage. Then circle the letter of the answer to each question.

Frostbite occurs when areas of the body are overexposed to extreme cold. Ice
crystals form in the tissues and restrict blood flow to the affected area. The parts
of the body that are most frequently affected by frostbite include the toes, fingers,
nose, and ears. The first sign that you are experiencing frostbite is that the skin of
the exposed area has turned very pale or grayish-blue. The body part feels cold and
is painful when touched. As the frostbite progresses, the damaged area becomes
numb. To treat frostbite, restore circulation and warmth to the affected area as
quickly as possible. Avoid using hot water bottles, heating pads, or heat lamps
because the temperatures of these items are too extreme. Instead, handle frostbitten
skin very gently and thaw skin tissue by soaking the area in warm—not hot—water
(102°F to 105°F). Finally, place gauze or cloth between fingers or toes before loosely
bandaging them. For serious frostbite, seek medical attention because extensive
tissue damage may have occurred.

1. You can conclude that frostbite should never be treated with a hot water bottle, heating pad, or heat
   lamp because

   A such treatment might produce temperatures that can damage frostbitten tissue.

   B such treatment will put the victim into shock.

   C it would take too long to thaw tissues using this kind of treatment.

   D most people do not have access to this kind of treatment.

2. How does frostbite affect the body?

   F The skin cracks, and the victim bleeds to death.

   G A victim's body temperature rises to between 102°F and 105°F.

   H Affected body parts become brittle.

   J Ice crystals form in the tissues and restrict blood flow to affected areas.

3. What should you do after you soak the frostbitten areas in warm water?

   A use a heat lamp to warm the body parts

   B use a hot water bottle

   C rub frostbitten areas briskly

   D place gauze or cloth between fingers or toes

4. What is the purpose of soaking the affected area in warm water?

   F to keep infection from spreading

   G to thaw the tissues

   H to clean the damaged skin

   J to relax the victim

What does a stick of dynamite have to do with the world's most famous prize? The story dates back to the 19th century and surrounds Alfred Nobel, a Swedish chemist and engineer. The Nobel family owned an explosives plant in which both Alfred and his younger brother worked. Alfred later built a factory to manufacture nitroglycerin, a highly explosive liquid. After a number of blasts occurred at the factory, Swedish authorities forced Nobel to move his operation outside the city. He began experimenting with adding various substances to nitroglycerin to make it easier to handle. In 1867 Nobel was granted a patent for a new explosive, which he called "dynamite." Although the invention of dynamite turned Alfred Nobel into a rich man, he was not always happy. He had little contact with other people and suffered frequent bouts of depression. When Nobel died, his will stipulated that the majority of his fortune be used to fund annual prizes in physics, chemistry, literature, medicine, and peace. The Nobel Prizes are the most respected prizes awarded.

5. What caused Nobel to move his work outside Stockholm?

   A Taxes in the city were too high.

   B There was too much air pollution, and he had trouble breathing.

   C Swedish authorities forced him to move after too many explosions.

   D The factory was too large to fit in the city limits.

6. Which of these is an opinion?

   F He suffered frequent bouts of depression.

   G The invention of dynamite turned Alfred Nobel into a rich man.

   H The Nobel Prizes are the most respected prizes awarded.

   J In 1867 he was granted a patent for dynamite.

7. What was the author's purpose for writing this passage?

   A to persuade people to use dynamite

   B to inform readers about the man who established the Nobel Prizes

   C to instruct readers in the correct procedure for using dynamite

   D to describe what it feels like to win a Nobel Prize

8. What is the best paraphrase of the last two sentences?

   F Nobel created prizes when he died. His will gave instructions for prizes to be established.

   G The most respected prizes in the world were established by Nobel's last will. It awards prizes in a number of categories.

   H In his will, Nobel created respected awards with his large fortune. The annual prizes are awarded in physics, chemistry, literature, medicine, and peace.

   J Nobel used his fortune to fund prizes in many subjects.

Pretest continued

> Some of the world's greatest discoveries were made purely by chance. For example, Sir Isaac Newton, the English mathematician and physicist, first understood the force of gravity when he observed an apple fall from a tree. At the same time, Newton noticed the crescent moon in the night sky. He began to wonder whether the same force that pulled the apple to the ground held the moon near Earth. Newton himself admitted that while the apple helped him to understand the force of gravity, it did not, as some people believe, fall and hit him on the head.

9. What is the main idea of this passage?

   A Sir Isaac Newton came upon the idea of gravity after observing an apple fall from a tree and relating it to the force that holds the moon near Earth.

   B Most scientific discoveries aren't true.

   C The story of how Sir Isaac Newton discovered gravity is exaggerated.

   D Sir Isaac Newton wondered how the moon stayed near Earth.

10. Which reference source might have this passage in it?

   F a dictionary

   G a novel

   H a magazine article

   J a government report

Read the section of a brochure about a cleaning service. Then circle the letter of the answer to each question.

> Happy Helpers is a fully licensed, bonded, and insured cleaning service. We provide the help you need to keep your home clean and tidy. Two cleaners will visit your home as frequently as you desire. If for some reason one of your regular helpers is unavailable, the Happy Helpers office will contact you in advance and offer to send a substitute helper. Problems or concerns about our employees or the quality of their work should be brought to our attention immediately, and we will work with you to remedy the situation. Give Happy Helpers a try today!

11. What should you do if you have a problem with the Happy Helpers cleaners?

   A Call the office.

   B Leave a note for the cleaners the next time they come.

   C Call and cancel your service.

   D Scold the cleaners.

12. Why is it important that the cleaning service be insured?

   F It helps you get better rates.

   G It makes the cleaning people work faster.

   H They need insurance if more than one person will be cleaning a home.

   J They will replace anything that is stolen or damaged.

Read each passage. Then circle the letter of the answer to each question.

---

(1) Chaske laced up his skates, pulling the laces so tight they strained the dark leather of the boot. (2) The left one was too big, the right one was too small, and his socks were bunched up under the arch of his foot. (3) He shivered in his light button-down shirt and wished he had worn a sweater. (4) He had expected the rink to be warm, but it was as cold as the inside of a refrigerator. (5) He stood up, arms flailing as he tried to keep his balance, all the while imagining Kaya's disgust. (6) He never should have agreed to go ice skating on their first date; he should have insisted on bowling. (7) Just then, Kaya walked over, perfectly balanced on her delicate white skates. (8) Smiling, she took Chaske's hand and began telling him about all the times she fell when she first learned to skate.

---

13. Which style technique is used in sentence 4?

  A simile

  B metaphor

  C personification

  D dialogue

14. What character trait does Kaya show?

  F carelessness

  G fear

  H kindness

  J stupidity

15. What is the genre or subgenre of this passage?

  A fiction

  B drama

  C poetry

  D letter

16. What effect is created by the author's writing style?

  F dreaminess

  G anger

  H delight

  J tension

Virgil's Foods is a terrible place to shop. For one thing, the staff is completely unhelpful and is sometimes downright rude to customers. Worse still, it's not uncommon to find food that has gone bad. I suggest that if you plan to buy cheese or other foods from Virgil's, you check the expiration dates carefully. The owner has been known to pull expired foods from the trash and return them to the shelf for purchase. The most frustrating thing is that no matter how many times the health inspector finds health-code violations in the store, the owner continues this disgusting practice.

---

17. What technique does the writer use to support the opinion, "Virgil's Foods is a terrible place to shop"?

  A using several unrelated examples

  B using statistics

  C describing the types of food the store sells

  D tracing the decline of the store over several years

18. The writer's intention for writing this passage is

  F to convince the health department to shut down the store.

  G to describe how it feels to work at Virgil's Foods.

  H to convey his or her disgust with Virgil's Foods.

  J to increase business to Virgil's Foods.

Many types of aquatic birds live near lakes, rivers, and oceans. While these birds do walk on land, they spend most of their time in the water, and with good reason. Penguins, for example, have squat legs and waddle from side to side. However, they can glide through the water with ease because their bodies are shaped like torpedoes. Ducks, another water bird, have webbed feet that act like paddles. Their legs, set wide and far back on their bodies, make their movement on land awkward.

19. You can generalize that all aquatic birds

- **A** have bodies shaped like torpedoes.
- **B** can't walk on land.
- **C** have bodies that are made for the water and are clumsy on land.
- **D** have squat legs that help them walk gracefully.

20. As used in this passage, the word *aquatic* means

- **F** "land-dwelling."
- **G** "flightless."
- **H** "living in or near water."
- **J** "made of water."

Study the map. Then circle the letter of the answer to each question.

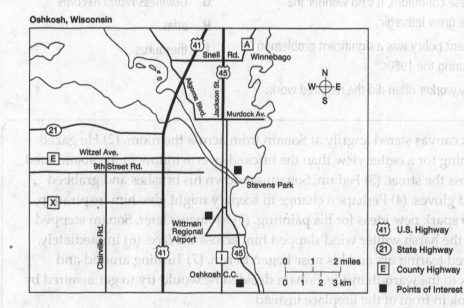

Oshkosh, Wisconsin

21. Lee lives at the corner of Clairville Road and 9th Street Road. Which way should he drive to get to Winnebago?

- **A** west on State Highway 21
- **B** north on U.S. Highway 41
- **C** south on County Highway I
- **D** west on Witzel Avenue

22. About how far is it from the Oshkosh C. C. to Stevens Park?

- **F** 4 miles
- **G** 8 miles
- **H** 16 miles
- **J** 1 mile

Pretest continued

Read each passage. Then circle the letter of the answer to each question.

> Employment policy was a significant problem in Poland during the 1980s. During this time, the Communist government insisted that state-owned businesses hire additional workers even when there was no work for them to do. One lucky worker often did the required work. Others watched or wasted time until the workday was done. Under these conditions, it's no wonder the workforce grew lethargic.

23. What caused the workforce to become lethargic?

A They didn't like Communism.

B There were too many workers for each job.

C They disliked working for the state.

D They didn't understand what they should be doing.

24. Which sentence is a fact?

F The Communist government insisted that state-owned businesses hire additional workers.

G Under these conditions, it's no wonder the workforce grew lethargic.

H Employment policy was a significant problem in Poland during the 1980s.

J One lucky worker often did the required work.

25. What is the genre or subgenre of this passage?

A mystery

B poetry

C essay

D romance

26. In what kind of reference source could you find a passage similar to this one?

F encyclopedia

G *Guinness World Records*

H atlas

J thesaurus

> (1) The blank canvas stared angrily at Sonam from across the room. (2) He gazed outside, wishing for a better view than the bricked-over window in the abandoned building across the street. (3) Fed up, Sonam set down his brushes and grabbed his jacket and gloves. (4) Perhaps a change in scenery might give him inspiration, something to spark new ideas for his painting. (5) Moments later, Sonam stepped outside, and the harsh winter wind slapped him across the face. (6) Immediately, his eyes started tearing up, and his nose began to run. (7) Turning around and running back to the warmth inside, Sonam decided he would try to get inspired by reading a book in front of the fireplace instead.

27. As used in the passage, *inspiration* means

A something that stimulates creativity.

B a cold, rough wind.

C general sickness or discomfort.

D new paint brushes.

28. What style technique does the author use in sentences 1 and 5?

F metaphor

G personification

H action

J dialogue

Pretest continued

Read this section of a workplace document explaining how to paint stripes on roads following repair or construction. Then circle the letter of the answer to each question.

- Check weather before painting. Paint should never be applied during rain or fog. These weather conditions could damage the freshly painted surface.
- Check condition of pavement before painting. Pavement should be clean and dry.
- Check that stripes meet the following conditions:
  - correct width and edge definition
  - correct length of stripes and gaps between stripes
  - correct alignment
  - second coat of paint aligns with first coat
- Drips, overspray, or incorrect markings must be removed after painting.

29. According to the document, what effect might occur if paint is applied in the rain?
  - **A** The equipment will be damaged.
  - **B** The painted surface will be damaged.
  - **C** The paint will not stick.
  - **D** The paint will look messy and not conform to standards.

30. What should workers do if there are paint drips?
  - **F** Wait for them to wear off naturally.
  - **G** Remove all paint and start over.
  - **H** Apply black tape over the drips.
  - **J** Remove the drips.

31. What is the best paraphrase of the last bullet?
  - **A** Spray over incorrect markings or drips.
  - **B** After painting, cover drips and overspray with tape.
  - **C** Remove any paint that is not correctly applied, including overspray and drips.
  - **D** If one stripe is incorrect, remove the stripes next to it.

32. What should you do before you paint?
  - **F** Check the condition of the pavement.
  - **G** Remove drips.
  - **H** Remove overspray.
  - **J** Check the color of the paint.

33. What do you think the author's purpose was for writing this document?
  - **A** to describe the correct width and length for road stripes
  - **B** to give an overview of how to correctly paint stripes on roads
  - **C** to describe the job of road-stripe painter for a want ad
  - **D** to explain when road stripes need repainting

34. What conclusion can you draw about painting stripes on roads?
  - **F** It is important to paint them neatly and correctly.
  - **G** As long as they are close to specifications, it does not matter if they are messy.
  - **H** The most important thing is to get them painted quickly.
  - **J** You should paint stripes as early as possible.

Read the workplace document. Then circle the letter of the answer to each question.

Envelope Manufacture

Empire State Envelope (Newburgh, NY)

A Newburgh envelope company is looking to fill the following positions:

Operators RO, 102, 527, Classic envelope folding machines

Responsibilities include basic operations of machines. Must be able to keep up with envelope production levels and quality standards. Accurate measurement and basic math skills required.

Adjusters RO, 102, 527, Classic envelope folding machines

MUST have experience on folding equipment.

Responsibilities include equipment setup, routine maintenance, troubleshooting equipment problems, and keeping up with envelope production levels and quality standards.

Positions are full-time with benefits. Openings are for first and third shifts. To apply, call 555-1245 or apply in person at the plant on Friday, February 10, from noon to 4 P.M.

---

35. What is one way in which the operator is different from the adjuster?

  A The operator must work on RO, 102, and 527 machines, while the adjuster only works on classic machines.

  B The operator needs to be able to keep up with production levels, but the adjuster does not.

  C The adjuster needs prior experience on folding machines, but the operator does not.

  D The adjuster is responsible for meeting quality standards, but the operator is not.

36. What is the difference in salary for the positions?

  F $5.00 per hour

  G $15.00 per hour

  H $20.00 per hour

  J not stated

37. You apply for a job here. You have good math and measurement skills but have never worked with a folding machine. What do you predict will happen?

  A You will be considered for a job as an operator.

  B You will be considered for a job as an adjuster.

  C You will not be a candidate for any job.

  D You will be given your choice of either job.

38. What do you think the author's purpose was for writing this ad?

  F to find out how many people know how to use folding machines

  G to fill operator and adjuster positions

  H to create descriptions of various positions for the company handbook

  J to inform HR that certain positions need to be filled

39. You want to apply in person for the operator job. What reference source could you use to find out where to go?

  A encyclopedia

  B almanac

  C phone book

  D dictionary

40. Which of these is NOT a responsibility of the adjuster?

  F troubleshooting equipment problems

  G equipment setup

  H overseeing operators

  J routine maintenance

Pretest continued

Circle the letter of the answer to each question.

41. Which word means the opposite of the underlined word?

glossy coat

- **A** shiny
- **B** dull
- **C** red
- **D** long

42. Which word does NOT belong in the word family?

- **F** preview
- **G** variable
- **H** overview
- **J** viewer

43. Which word means "the most friendly"?

- **A** friendlyer
- **B** friendlyest
- **C** friendlier
- **D** friendliest

44. Which two words are homophones?

- **F** cancel, conceal
- **G** garage, garbage
- **H** remark, remake
- **J** build, billed

45. What is the correct contraction of *he would*?

- **A** he'ould
- **B** he'd
- **C** hew'ld
- **D** hed'd

46. Which word means the same or almost the same as the underlined word?

sour lemon

- **F** sweet
- **G** tart
- **H** salty
- **J** tasty

47. Which word fits into both sentences?

Amado threw a _____ for his dog to fetch.

Hsiu Mei used glue to _____ her photos onto the collage.

- **A** toy
- **B** place
- **C** ball
- **D** stick

48. Which word means "having three angles"?

- **F** semiangle
- **G** biangle
- **H** uniangle
- **J** triangle

49. Which word is the plural of the word *branch*?

- **A** branchs
- **B** branches
- **C** branchies
- **D** branves

50. Which word means "having the quality of envy"?

- **F** envyious
- **G** envyous
- **H** envous
- **J** envious

51. Which word means "behave badly"?

- **A** unbehave
- **B** disbehave
- **C** misbehave
- **D** nonbehave

52. Which word means "like a child"?

- **F** childic
- **G** childish
- **H** childive
- **J** childious

53. Which phrase means "the brushes belonging to Carmela"?

A Carmelas brushes'

B Carmelas' brushes

C Carmela's brushes

D Carmela brushe's

54. Which word fits into both sentences?

The actress panicked and forgot her _____.

Zahur arranged his shoes in a _____ in his closet.

F part

G arrange

H match

J line

55. Which word means "the result of being confused"?

A confusion

B confusing

C confused

D confution

56. Which word means "partly conscious"?

F semiconscious

G unconscious

H subconscious

J consciously

57. What is the meaning of the word *comical*?

A partly comedy

B having the characteristics of comedy

C a person who practices comedy

D the most comedy

58. Which word means "to make tangled"?

F retangle

G entangle

H mistangle

J untangle

59. Which word means "to play again"?

A subplay

B unplay

C deplay

D replay

60. Which word completes the analogy?

ox : oxen as *deer* :

F deer

G deers

H meadow

J woods

61. Which word means "to weave between"?

A superweave

B interweave

C multiweave

D subweave

62. Which is the plural form of the word *elf?*

F elfs

G elfes

H elvs

J elves

63. Which word means the opposite of the underlined word?

ancient ruin

A well-known

B old

C modern

D beautiful

64. Which word means "a person who plays the violin"?

F violiner

G violinist

H violor

J violist

This pretest was designed to help you determine which reading skills you need to study. This chart shows which skill is being covered with each test question. Use the key on page 12 to check your answers. Then circle the questions you answered incorrectly and go to the practice pages in this book covering those skills.

Tested Skills	Question Numbers	Practice Pages
Recognize and Recall Details	4, 30, 40	14–17
Stated and Implied Concepts	2, 36	22–25
Draw Conclusions	1, 12, 34	30–33
Summarize and Paraphrase	8, 31	38–41
Identify Cause and Effect	5, 23, 29	46–49
Understand Author's Purpose	7, 33, 38	54–57
Find the Main Idea	9	62–65
Identify Sequence	3, 32	78–81
Understand Consumer Materials	11, 12	86–89
Use Reference Sources/Maps	10, 21, 22, 26, 39	94–97
Use Supporting Evidence	17	102–105
Recognize Character Traits	14	110–113
Identify Style Techniques	13, 28	118–121
Make Generalizations	19	134–137
Author's Effect and Intention	16, 18	142–145
Compare and Contrast	35	150–153
Predict Outcomes	37	158–161
Identify Fact and Opinion	6, 24	166–169
Identify Genre	15, 25	174–177
Spelling	44, 45, 49, 53, 62	20, 28, 44, 45, 52, 60, 108, 157, 181
Synonyms/Antonyms	41, 46, 63	37, 124, 140, 148
Context Clues	20, 27, 47, 54	21, 53, 69, 85, 101, 117, 173
Word Analysis	42, 43, 48, 50, 51, 52, 55–61, 64	20, 29, 36, 44, 52, 60, 61, 68, 84, 92, 93, 100, 108, 109, 116, 124, 125, 140, 141, 148, 149, 156, 164, 165, 172, 180

KEY			
1.	A	33.	B
2.	J	34.	F
3.	D	35.	C
4.	G	36.	J
5.	C	37.	A
6.	H	38.	G
7.	B	39.	C
8.	H	40.	H
9.	A	41.	B
10.	H	42.	G
11.	A	43.	D
12.	J	44.	J
13.	A	45.	B
14.	H	46.	G
15.	A	47.	D
16.	J	48.	J
17.	A	49.	B
18.	H	50.	J
19.	C	51.	C
20.	H	52.	G
21.	B	53.	C
22.	F	54.	J
23.	B	55.	A
24.	F	56.	F
25.	C	57.	B
26.	F	58.	G
27.	A	59.	D
28.	G	60.	F
29.	B	61.	B
30.	J	62.	J
31.	C	63.	C
32.	F	64.	G

Unit 1

In this unit you will learn how to

You will practice the following workplace skills

You will also learn new words and their meanings and put your reading skills to work in written activities. You will get additional reading practice in *Reading Basics Advanced Reader*.

Lesson 1.1

Recognize and Recall Details

Details are words and phrases that give information in a piece of writing. They are the facts or explanations that give more information about the main ideas of a text or provide extra information that is interesting to the reader. Details can be examples, descriptions, statistical data, or opinions of people knowledgeable about the topic. An writer will use a variety of supporting details to strengthen an argument, defend a viewpoint, explain a topic, or create a vivid description. To identify the supporting details, ask yourself this question: What evidence or proof is offered to help me better understand the writer's viewpoint or the topic?

The reading technique of scanning can help you locate details in a passage. After you initially read the passage, you scan it by rereading it quickly but closely to find a specific fact or detail. As you read, concentrate only on finding the piece of information for which you are looking. Taking notes as you read will help you recall details. Read to find the U.S. gross domestic product for 2008 in this example:

> A country's gross domestic product (GDP) measures the value of all goods and services produced by every economy each year. Using this standard, the U.S. GDP was about $14 trillion in 2008, roughly double the GDP of the next closest country, China.

The example gives details about the U.S. gross domestic product for a certain year. If you underline, highlight, or make a note in a notebook about the detail, $14 trillion, you can find it more easily when you need to review the passage. If you are asked a question related to this detail, such as, "How does China's GDP compare to the U.S. GDP?" you can scan the text surrounding the detail to find information quickly.

Read the passage to find out what can happen to astronauts' hearts if they experience long-term space travel. Underline the detail.

> Scientists have been studying the harmful physical effects of long-term space travel. When astronauts spend many weeks in space, their muscles often become weak, and their bones lose calcium, an important mineral. Pulse rates have been found to increase because the heart can shrink by about 10 percent. Fatigue from space flight also disturbs sleep.

Did you find that hearts can shrink about 10 percent? The detail about heart shrinkage is in the third sentence. It explains why pulse rates increase and supports the idea that long-term space travel can be harmful to the body.

Read each passage. Then answer the questions.

The work of several scientists led to the modern model of the atom. As is often the case, each scientist built on the work of others. In 1803 John Dalton suggested that atoms were solid, but further experiments showed that this was incorrect. In 1898 J. J. Thomson showed that atoms contained electrons. Further work improved on this model, and later, experiments by Ernest Rutherford showed that atoms were made of a dense, positively charged nucleus surrounded by negative electrons.

1. Which three scientists are credited in the passage with establishing the modern model of the atom?

_____

2. What was Thomson's contribution to understanding the atom?

_____

_____

3. In what year did Dalton make his suggestion about atoms? _____

In the 1800s most people who worked in the city also lived there because it was difficult to travel long distances. Modern transportation methods—such as trains, trolleys, and later, automobiles—allowed people to work in one place and live in another. Interstate highways also made it easier for people to travel from outlying, or surrounding, areas to the cities. With the highways came the trucking industry. Trucking allowed industries to be located outside cities because the industries no longer needed to be close to railroads in order to ship their goods.

4. What three modern transportation methods are mentioned in the passage?

_____

5. According to the writer, what allowed industries to be located away from railroads?

_____

_____

6. Which innovation led to the development of the trucking industry?

_____

Read each passage. Underline the main idea. Then find details in the passage that support the main idea. List the details on the lines.

> News about large businesses grabs most of the headlines, but small businesses are an important part of the American economy. Generally speaking, a small business is a firm that employs fewer than 500 workers. In 2002 more than 99 percent of U.S. businesses were small businesses, and these small firms created over two-thirds of all new jobs. They also produced about one-half of the country's output of goods and services. Keeping small businesses healthy is important for U.S. economic prosperity.

1. _____

2. _____

3. _____

4. _____

> You can take a few simple steps to prepare your car for the harsh conditions of winter. First, change the antifreeze to prevent the water that cools your engine from freezing. Then, check that your heater and defroster are in good working order. Examine the treads on your tires to ensure that they have not worn down too much. Make sure you have enough windshield-wiper fluid to keep your windshield clean, and check it often. In winter the dirty slush ends up on your windshield whenever another vehicle passes, and it's important to clean it off so you can see. Finally, check that you have a good ice scraper, snow brush, and extra gloves in the car.

5. _____

6. _____

7. _____

8. _____

9. _____

10. _____

Read the passage. Then circle the letter of the answer to each question.

There are two main types of trees, coniferous and deciduous. Coniferous trees, whose name derives from their cones, look the same throughout the year. Most of these trees have needlelike leaves that don't fall off in the winter and live in temperate regions. Two exceptions are the larches and the bald cypress, which shed their needles for winter. Coniferous trees are pine trees and their relatives, including spruce, fir, and hemlock trees.

Deciduous trees, which are also called broad-leaved trees, change throughout the year. Their leaves fall off in autumn, so the branches are bare in winter. Most deciduous leaves turn bright colors before they fall off. Maples, for example, usually turn red, while tulip poplars turn yellow. There are hundreds of species of deciduous trees, including oaks, maples, beeches, and poplars.

1. Which are the two types of trees mentioned in this passage?

   A coniferous and fruit-bearing

   B coniferous and deciduous

   C date and fig

   D deciduous and palm

2. How many different species of deciduous trees are there?

   F hundreds

   G millions

   H 351

   J none

3. Which is a type of coniferous tree?

   A maple

   B oak

   C hemlock

   D poplar

4. Oaks, beeches, and maples are examples of which type of tree?

   F hemlock

   G coniferous

   H pine

   J deciduous

5. Which are coniferous trees that shed their needles in the winter?

   A hemlock and fir

   B larch and bald cypress

   C maple and beech

   D No coniferous trees shed their needles.

6. Which tree's leaves usually turn yellow in the fall?

   F tulip poplars

   G oak

   H poplar

   J beech

7. What color do maple leaves usually turn before falling off?

   A white

   B yellow

   C red

   D Maple leaves do not change color before they fall off.

8. Which is a type of deciduous tree?

   F bald cypress

   G spruce

   H poplar

   J larch

Workplace Skill:
Recognize Details in a Request for Proposal

A request for proposal is an invitation for suppliers to submit a proposal on a specific commodity or service. To understand a request for proposal, you need to pay attention to the details. To better understand what you read, look for the facts, statistics, examples, and reasons that support or describe the main idea.

Read the request for proposal. Then circle the letter of the answer to each question below the box.

RFP 72-10 Riverside Mall Food Court Concession Stand

General Information

This request for proposal must be signed by someone with the authority to create proposals. The person must also be able to take part in contract negotiations. Submittals must follow this RFP.

Submittal Criteria

Please include the following:

1. the names and responsibilities of all persons who will be providing services
2. a statement of experience in providing food services
3. a menu that lists prices for all food and drinks
4. suggested hours of operation
5. a maintenance and cleaning plan
6. suggested payment to Riverside Mall for use of the facilities and right to sell food and drink

1. Who must sign the request for proposal?

   A   a representative from Riverside Mall

   B   the person providing all food services

   C   a person with the authority to create proposals

   D   a person in charge of the maintenance and cleaning plan

2. What does RFP stand for?

   F   Riverside food preparation

   G   request for proposal

   H   Riverside food proposal

   J   rental food property

3. The request for proposal must include the names of

   A   the owner and the manager.

   B   all persons providing services.

   C   the owner and the mall representative.

   D   the person responsible for payment.

4. Which is NOT required for the submittal?

   F   a maintenance and cleaning plan

   G   suggested hours of operation

   H   a nutrition guide for all food and drinks

   J   a menu that lists prices for all food and drinks

Write for Work

Imagine you are submitting an RFP to provide food service at Riverside Mall. In a notebook, write a statement that describes your experience and qualifications in food service. Make sure to include specific details to meet the submittal criteria, including dates, responsibilities, reasons you are qualified, and examples of your experience.

  Reading Extension

Turn to "Secret Service Agents: Shield, Defend, Protect" on page 1 of *Reading Basics Advanced Reader*. After you have read and/or listened to the article, answer the questions below.

Circle the letter of the answer to each question.

1. Who established the Secret Service?

  A Abraham Lincoln

  B William McKinley

  C John F. Kennedy

  D Ronald Reagan

2. When the Secret Service was first established, what was its primary purpose?

  F to protect the president

  G to track down counterfeiters

  H to protect visiting officials

  J to provide intelligence

3. Which president did Tim McCarthy protect?

  A Abraham Lincoln

  B William McKinley

  C John F. Kennedy

  D Ronald Reagan

4. Which secret service agent was responsible for getting President Reagan into the car after he was shot?

  F Tim McCarthy

  G Clinton Hill

  H Jerry Parr

  J James Huse Jr.

Write the answer to each question.

5. What is one way that the Secret Service tightened security after Kennedy was assassinated?

_____

_____

6. Name some personality traits that Secret Service agents must possess.

_____

_____

_____

Explore Words

Write for Work

PREFIXES

A prefix is a word part that can be added to the beginning of many words. Adding a prefix changes the meaning of the word to which it is added. Here are some common prefixes, their meanings, and examples:

mis-	"wrong" or "badly"	*mistreats* (treats badly)
dis-	"not" or "the opposite of"	*disagree* (the opposite of *agree*)
un-	"not" or "the opposite of"	*uncomfortable* (not comfortable)
non-	"not" or "the opposite of"	*nonprofit* (not for profit)

Read each phrase. Using one of the prefixes above, write a word with the same meaning as the phrase. Then write a brief sentence using the new word.

1. heard incorrectly _____

2. the opposite of *abilities* _____

3. not toxic _____

4. not believable _____

5. spelled wrong _____

SPELLING: PLURALS

Plural nouns are nouns that name more than one person, place, or thing. Some spelling rules apply when forming plurals.

- To make most nouns plural, add *-s* to the end of the word (*student/students*).
- To form the plural of words that end with *s, ss, sh, x,* or *ch,* add *-es* (*boss/bosses*).
- For words that end in *y,* change the *y* to *i* and add *-es* (*penny/pennies*).
- For most words that end in *f* or *ff,* add *-s* to form the plural (*chiefs, spoofs, staffs*).
- For some words that end in *f,* change the final *f* to *ves* (*half/halves; wolf/wolves*).
- For words that end in *-fe,* first change the *f* to *v* and then add *-s* (*wife/wives*).

Write the plural of each word on the line.

1. country _____

2. scarf _____

3. cockroach _____

4. blemish _____

5. life _____

6. roof _____

CONTEXT CLUES

When you read, you will come across some unfamiliar words. You can usually figure out their meaning by using context. Context is other words, phrases, and sentences that surround the unfamiliar word and give you clues to the word's meaning.

Use context clues to figure out the meaning of each underlined word. Write the meaning.

1. The disappearance of the ocean liner *Waratah* is a mystery in nautical history.

Your definition: _____

2. The ship left the port of Durban, South Africa, in 1909, bound for Cape Town.

Your definition: _____

3. At some point in the voyage, the ship vanished without a trace.

Your definition: _____

4. Searchers found neither survivors nor flotsam.

Your definition: _____

5. To this day, no one has been able to offer a plausible explanation.

Your definition: _____

ACADEMIC VOCABULARY

Knowing these high-frequency words will help you in many school subjects.

recall   to remember a fact

detail   an individual feature, fact, or item

economy   the wealth and resources of a country or place

standard   something used as a measure

output   the amount of something produced by a person or industry

Complete the sentences below using one of the words above.

1. Loto wrote down every _____ she could remember about the accident.

2. The country's _____ is on the rise.

3. The cloth factory's _____ has increased since it bought better machinery.

4. It was hard for Jimena to _____ many details about her preschool.

5. Lomasi's beautiful performances set the _____ for every musician that came after him.

Lesson 1.2

Understand Stated and Implied Concepts

When you read, it is important to understand the ideas and concepts that are presented in the text. A stated concept is information that the writer gives directly. Stated concepts are often supported or clarified by details, which provide additional facts, reasons, or examples. To understand an implied concept, you must compare the information in the passage with your own knowledge, opinions, and experiences.

In most selections, some important ideas are stated directly, while others are implied. It is important to distinguish between stated and implied concepts. Knowing which ideas were directly stated will help you understand what you have read. It will also help you distinguish which ideas came from the text and which ideas you inferred. Read the example and look for stated and implied concepts.

(1) Many people would be surprised to learn that mold offers many benefits. (2) For example, blue cheese is made with a blue mold, which gives the cheese its tangy flavor. (3) Penicillin is also a mold—a very powerful one that cures infections and often saves lives.

Sentences 2 and 3 directly state that mold is used in making blue cheese and penicillin. Sentence 1 includes an implied concept: most people think of mold as a bad thing.

Many selections that you read will present new information and include unfamiliar words and concepts. It is very likely that you will need to read some passages several times to understand all the stated and implied concepts that are presented.

Read the passage. Underline the sentence that states why the Pony Express became obsolete.

> The Pony Express has been romanticized in tales about the early western United States, but it actually played an extremely practical role. It was begun in 1860 to carry mail between Missouri and California using the fastest mode of communication available—a man on a horse. A route was a kind of relay race across the country. There were relief stations about every 15 miles to give the rider food, water, and a fresh horse. After riding for about 75 miles, the messenger handed his mail pouch to the next man in the relay, who continued the route. The Pony Express became obsolete when it had to compete with new technology—the telegraph.

Did you underline "The Pony Express became obsolete when it had to compete with new technology—the telegraph"? That sentence states the information directly: the Pony Express became obsolete, or outdated, when the telegraph came into use.

Read the passage. Then read each statement that follows. If the concept is stated directly in the passage, circle *stated*. If the concept is not stated directly but is implied, circle *implied*. If there is no evidence to support the concept, circle *not known*.

In A.D. 79 the city of Pompeii, Italy, was a resort for wealthy Roman citizens. The city had been constructed next to a volcano—Mount Vesuvius. Although the volcano had been dormant, it erupted one day, throwing fiery ash and stone on the city and filling the air with poisonous gas. Pompeii was destroyed—buried under many feet of cinder and ash. Scientists have uncovered the ruins of Pompeii and have found the remains of about 2,000 people. The shapes of their bodies were preserved like shells by hardened ash. Scientists have restored many of the ancient temples and palaces so that modern tourists can stroll through the streets of this once great but doomed city.

1. Pompeii was a city in Italy.

stated   implied   not known

2. Pompeii was a place where wealthy people went to relax.

stated   implied   not known

3. No one expected Mount Vesuvius to erupt.

stated   implied   not known

4. Pompeii was buried under cinders and hot ash.

stated   implied   not known

5. The air was filled with poisonous gas from the volcano.

stated   implied   not known

6. Hot lava flowed through the streets of Pompeii and into people's homes.

stated   implied   not known

7. The volcanic eruption lasted for two entire days.

stated   implied   not known

8. Today Pompeii is a popular tourist destination.

stated   implied   not known

9. Scientists found the remains of about 2,000 people that were preserved by ash.

stated   implied   not known

Read each passage. Then answer the questions.

(1) Scientists are still not sure why dinosaurs vanished from Earth. (2) One theory is that a change in climate caused their disappearance. (3) Before the great beasts became extinct more than 60 million years ago, Earth was a tropical planet, so it was much warmer and wetter than it is today. (4) Scientists think that as Earth's temperatures dropped, the tropical vegetation was destroyed. (5) The herbivores, or plant-eating dinosaurs, would then have followed the plants to extinction. (6) In turn, this development would have left the carnivores, or meat-eating dinosaurs, without their food source.

1. Which sentence states what may have caused the dinosaurs to become extinct? _____

2. Which sentence states how long ago the dinosaurs became extinct? _____

3. Which sentence states the meaning of the word *herbivore*? _____

4. Which sentence states the meaning of the word *carnivore*? _____

5. What concept about the carnivores' diet is implied by the passage?

_____

_____

(1) In recorded history, the earthquake stands out as one of the most destructive forces in nature. (2) An incredibly destructive quake occurred in 1556 in Shensi Province, China. (3) That disaster took the lives of 830,000 people. (4) In 1923 another severe quake struck in the Kanto Plain in Japan, destroying more than 600,000 dwellings in Tokyo and Yokohama and causing billions of dollars worth of damage.

6. Which sentence states the location of Shensi Province? _____

7. Which sentence states how many people died from the earthquake in 1556? _____

8. What concept is implied about the Kanto Plain earthquake from the passage?

_____

_____

Read the passage. Then circle the letter of the answer to each question.

> Today people can walk into a restaurant at practically any hour of the day or night and order just about whatever they want. It hasn't always been that way. Until the late 18th century, only inns served meals and only at scheduled times and with limited items. Customers had to arrive at the correct time and eat whatever meal the manager had decided to serve that day. This system was eventually changed in Paris, France, where sophisticated cuisine has long been considered an art form. As the story goes, in 1765 a place called Boulanger's was the first restaurant in Paris. It offered customers a menu that gave them a choice of several meals. Fifty years later, there were approximately 500 restaurants in Paris.

1. What was one difference between the way in which inns served meals before the 18th century and the way in which restaurants serve meals today?

   A Inns served one meal at a set time, but today you can get a meal at a restaurant at any time.

   B Inns served all kinds of food, but restaurants have limited menus.

   C Unlike today, the meals then were free.

   D The information is not stated in the passage.

2. In which city did the system change?

   F London

   G Paris

   H Los Angeles

   J The information is not stated in the passage.

3. What unusual feature did Boulanger's offer its customers?

   A tablecloths

   B waitresses

   C menus with choices

   D The information is not stated in the passage.

4. What type of meals did Boulanger's offer?

   F soups

   G beef entrees

   H chicken and fish

   J The information is not stated in the passage.

5. How many restaurants in Paris used menus by the early 1800s?

   A none

   B about 50

   C about 500

   D The information is not stated in the passage.

6. Who first suggested creating a menu of meal choices?

   F a customer

   G a manager

   H a restaurant owner

   J The information is not stated in the passage.

7. What prompted Boulanger's to create a menu of meal choices?

   A They wanted to get ahead of their competition.

   B They wanted to showcase the chef's talent.

   C They could not agree on what to serve.

   D The information is not stated in the passage.

8. What was the name of the first restaurant in London?

   F Boulanger's

   G Paris

   H Choice Inn

   J The information is not stated in the passage.

Workplace Skill:
Locate Stated and Implied Concepts in a Letter of Appointment

Companies create documents so that employees know what is expected of them in the workplace. For a complete understanding of what you read, you must identify the stated and implied concepts.

Read the letter of appointment. Then circle the letter of the answer to each question.

Dear Mudiwa Sow:

This is to confirm that you have been hired as a temporary employee in the Office of Business Administration at Weber Technical College, effective Monday, August 30. As a temporary worker, you are not eligible to receive benefits from Weber Technical College. You are not a permanent employee, and, therefore, you do not receive paid time off or paid holidays. Your temporary status does not entitle you to priority for regular full-time or permanent employment.

Temporary employees must adhere to the same rules, policies, and regulations as regular employees. To ensure the safety of all employees, background checks are conducted on all employees, including temporary employees.

We look forward to seeing you on Monday, August 30. Please report to the front office of the Business Administration Building at 7:30 A.M. to begin your assignment. If you have any questions or concerns, please do not hesitate to contact me.

Sincerely,

Kiyono Ito

Hiring Manager, Office of Business Administration

1. Which idea is directly stated in the first paragraph?

   A   A temporary position is a good job opportunity.

   B   Mudiwa Sow has the same benefits as a permanent employee.

   C   Weber Technical College has many job opportunities.

   D   Temporary employees do not receive paid time off.

2. A permanent position is available at Weber Technical College. You can conclude that Mudiwa Sow

   F   will get no special consideration.

   G   will become a permanent employee.

   H   will automatically be given an interview.

   J   will be eligible for the position without benefits.

Write the answer to the question.

3. What are some differences between a temporary employee at Weber Techical College and a permanent employee?

Write for Work

Imagine that you are Mudiwa Sow and have questions about the upcoming temporary assignment. In a notebook, write a letter to Kiyono Ito to ask three specific questions you have about your employment that were not addressed in your letter of appointment. For example, you might have questions about your specific responsibilities or documents you need to bring with you.

 Reading Extension

Turn to "Humanitarian Aid Workers: Comfort Under Fire" on page 9 of *Reading Basics Advanced Reader*. After you have read and/or listened to the article, answer the questions below.

Circle the letter of the answer to each question.

1. What aid work were Zarema Sadulayeva and Alik Djabrailov doing before they were killed?

   A They vaccinated people against malaria and polio.

   B They established clean water sources close to villages.

   C They delivered much-needed food and medicine.

   D They provided false limbs, surgery, and counseling to children.

2. Why does Charles Rogers think that the targeting of aid workers will increase?

   F The risks to aid workers are greatly exaggerated.

   G There are little or no consequences for those who kill aid workers.

   H There are not enough resources to protect aid workers.

   J No one can pinpoint which group attacks the workers or what side they are on.

Write the answer to each question.

3. Why did Karen Smith abandon her plan to breed racehorses?

   _____

   _____

4. What precautions does Smith take when she is in the field?

   _____

   _____

Explore Words

Write for Work

SPELLING: WORD ENDINGS

You can add endings to many words. When adding endings such as *-ed*, *-ing*, *-er*, and *-est*, some spelling rules apply:

- If a word ends in silent *e*, first drop the *e* and then add the ending, as in *stale, staler, stalest*.

- For most words that end in a vowel and one consonant, first double the consonant. Then add the ending, as in *submit, submitted, submitting*.

- For two-syllable words that are pronounced with the accent on the first syllable, just add the ending, as in *label, labeled, labeling*.

Add the ending to each word. Write the new word on the line.

1. stupid + est _____   **6.** refuse + ed _____

2. zigzag + ed _____   **7.** dispute + ing _____

3. upset + ing _____   **8.** repel + ed _____

4. fine + est _____   **9.** wise + er _____

5. confuse + ing _____   **10.** focus + ed _____

SPELLING: POSSESSIVES

Possessive words show that something belongs to one person or more than one person. Singular possessive words always include an apostrophe followed by *s* (*'s*). For example, the apartment where one cousin lives is *your cousin's apartment*. Plural possessive words include an *s* followed by an apostrophe (*s'*). For example, the apartment where two or more of your cousins live is *your cousins' apartment*.

Show ownership by writing a possessive phrase. Use *'s or s'*.

1. the house where my parents live _____

2. the dogs that my neighbor owns _____

3. the children of your brother _____

4. the party that my friends gave _____

5. the toy that belongs to the dog _____

6. the lunches that belong to the workers _____

Reading Basics · Advanced

SUFFIXES -er, -or, -ist

A suffix is a word part that can be added to the end of many words. Suffixes have meaning, and adding a suffix changes the meaning of a base word.

-er	"a person who"	*leader* (a person who leads)
-or	"a person who"	*instructor* (a person who instructs)
-ist	"a person who makes or practices"	*scientist* (someone who practices science)

Read each phrase. Using one of the suffixes above, write a word with the same meaning as the phrase. Then write a brief sentence using the new word.

1. a person who acts _____

2. people who wrestle _____

3. a person who practices psychology _____

4. people who make cartoons _____

5. a person who practices conservation _____

6. a person who landscapes _____

ACADEMIC VOCABULARY

Knowing these high-frequency words will help you in many school subjects.

distinguish	to perceive or recognize one from another
clarify	to make understandable
directly	in a clear, straightforward way
state	to say or tell
infer	to work out or decide something from evidence and reasoning rather than from direct statements

Complete the sentences below using one of the words above.

1. Witnesses in a courtroom are warned to _____ only the facts.

2. Rodrigo asked Daniella to _____ the meaning of the instructions.

3. We dressed the twins differently to help us _____ one from the other.

4. Many clues in the chapter helped me _____ that the waiter committed the crime.

5. The next week, Jorge asked her _____ if she'd like to have dinner with him.

Lesson 1.3

Draw Conclusions

INTRODUCE

A conclusion is a decision or opinion you form based on something you read or hear. Drawing a conclusion requires using several pieces of information to make a statement about people, places, events, and ideas. Readers combine stated and implied information from the text with prior knowledge to draw a conclusion.

Drawing a conclusion might be understood as putting information together in the following way:

> stated facts + implied facts + personal experience and knowledge = conclusion

Make sure your conclusions are not contradicted by anything in the text or by specific or general information you know to be true from your own experience. Read the example:

> Some studies show that people who take sleeping pills over long periods of time become irritable or depressed. One possible explanation is that sleeping pills inhibit normal dreaming.

If you concluded from this passage that sleeping pills are good for long-term use, your conclusion would be faulty. Rather, you should note that sleeping pills taken over long periods can make people irritable or depressed. A better conclusion would be that sleeping pills are good for short-term use only. When you draw conclusions, make sure they are based on facts.

Read the passage. Decide what conclusions you can draw about how minted coins have helped archaeologists know more about the kingdom of Aksum.

> The ancient African kingdom of Aksum was once located near the Red Sea in present-day Ethiopia. It was an important commerce center from about the first century B.C. to the seventh century A.D. Late in the third century A.D., Aksum followed the Roman practice of minting coins that had the ruler's name inscribed. One of the most important kings of Aksum was Ezana, who reigned during the fourth century. He led a campaign against another kingdom, Kush, and destroyed its capital.

One conclusion you can draw is that by studying the names on the coins, archaeologists can learn about the rulers of Aksum. Another conclusion you can draw from the presence and appearance of the minted coins is that Aksum was influenced by the practices of the Roman Empire.

Read each passage. Then read the conclusion drawn from the facts in the passage. Decide whether the conclusion is valid based on the facts. If it is valid, write *valid*. If it is not valid, write a new, valid conclusion.

> In 1865 writer Jules Verne's novel *From the Earth to the Moon* was published. In July 1969, 104 years later, *Apollo 11* landed on the moon. Both Verne's fictional launch site and the real-life NASA facilities are located in Florida. Verne's fictional launcher was called *Columbiad,* and the command module of the real spacecraft was called *Columbia*. The Verne expedition reached the moon in four days and one hour, and the real flight lasted about four days and seven hours. Finally, both Verne and NASA chose an ocean landing for the returning flight.

Conclusion: There are amazing similarities between Jules Verne's novel and the *Apollo 11* flight to the moon.

1. _____

_____

> American Christopher Latham Sholes helped design the first typewriter in 1867, but it wasn't all that practical. The typists could not see what they were typing, and the typewriter had no lowercase letters, no zero, and no one. The keys were arranged alphabetically, unlike the QWERTY arrangement that is familiar today.

Conclusion: The typewriter was a useless invention.

2. _____

_____

> During the Middle Ages, people were often highly superstitious, and anything out of the ordinary that happened was regarded with fear. For example, most people throughout history have been right-handed, and for that reason, left-handedness was regarded as an evil omen. The English word *sinister*, meaning "evil," comes from the Latin word for *sinister*, which meant both "left" and "unlucky."

Conclusion: Superstitions usually grow from fear.

3. _____

_____

Read each passage. Then answer each question.

In the 1600s American colonists made candles using animal fat and cotton. After bringing back a deer, moose, or bear from a hunting trip, they would boil the animal's fat in water. Then they would dip a piece of twisted cotton into the waxy substance that floated on the water's surface. When one layer hardened on the cotton wick, they dipped it again. The more the wick was dipped, the more wax stuck to it, until it became a useful, tapered candle.

1. What can you conclude about the daily lives of early American colonists?

_____

_____

Susan B. Anthony, born in 1820, was a pioneer of the women's suffrage movement. As a young woman, she worked to abolish drinking and slavery, but eventually she devoted most of her time to gaining voting rights for women. In 1869 Anthony cofounded the powerful National Woman Suffrage Association. In 1872 she went to the polls and voted in order to challenge laws that kept women from voting. She was arrested, tried, and convicted for this act. Anthony continued to work for women's suffrage until her death in 1906. In that year, only four states allowed women to vote, but in 1920, the Nineteenth Amendment to the Constitution granted women equal voting rights. Decades after her death, Anthony became the first woman to appear on American currency.

2. What can you conclude about Susan B. Anthony's contributions to women gaining the right to vote?

_____

_____

In the hot months of summer, some people use air conditioning to cool off. Air conditioners use electricity. Electric bills are based on the amount of electricity used by a household. They vary from month to month.

3. What can you conclude about the link between air conditioning and electric bills from this passage?

_____

_____

Read each passage. Then circle the letter of the answer to each question.

In ancient history, the kingfisher bird attracted attention because of its fantastic plumage. Ancient Tatar warriors supposedly believed that if they brushed a woman's skin with the bird's feathers, the woman would fall in love with them. The Chinese used the shiny blue feathers in their decorative screens.

1. From this passage you can conclude that the kingfisher

    A   is now extinct.

    B   excited the imagination of ancient cultures.

    C   has magical powers.

    D   is now raised mainly in captivity.

In the late 1400s Europeans first began to apply decorative paper to walls. The first wallpapers were inexpensive. They were hand-painted or stenciled to imitate the tapestries or wood paneling that was often found in the luxurious homes of the wealthy. Wallpapers went through an evolution in the 1600s when flocked wallpaper and painted Chinese papers became popular trends.

2. From this passage you can conclude that the first inexpensive wallpapers

    F   enabled the middle class to surpass the decor of the wealthy.

    G   were probably imported from China.

    H   duplicated formal landscapes.

    J   were used to make average people's homes look fancier.

Thomas Edison was an American inventor who is credited with the invention of the electric light bulb, the phonograph, and the movie camera and projector. By age 22 he was working in New York and had invented a new stock ticker. With the money from that patent, he opened up his own laboratory. After that, Edison spent almost all his time in his laboratory, devoting his time to inventing.

3. From this passage you can conclude that Thomas Edison

    A   never wanted to be an inventor at all.

    B   didn't care much about money.

    C   was a talented businessperson as well as an inventor.

    D   invented electricity.

Workplace Skill:
Draw Conclusions about a Table

Businesses use graphics, such as tables, diagrams, and graphs, to provide information in a visual format. When you use information in a text or graphic and your own knowledge to figure something out, you are drawing a conclusion. Drawing conclusions can help you figure out details that are not directly stated.

Study the table. Then circle the letter of the answer to each question below the box.

Industry	NAICS code	2008 Annual average employment (thousands)	Incidence rate	
			2007	2008
Fire protection (local government)	92216	227.4	_____	14.8
Police protection (local government)	92212	435.3		14.5
Skiing facilities (private industry)	71392	35.1	16.5	14.2
Secondary smelting and alloying of aluminum (private Industry)	331314	6.4	8.8	13.7
Steel foundries (except investment) (private industry)	331513	21.4	13.8	13.7
Sports teams and clubs (private industry)	711211	16.2	16.2	13.4

Highest Incidence Rates[1] of Total Nonfatal Occupational Injury and Illness Cases, 2008

1 The incidence rates represent the number of injuries and illnesses per 100 full-time workers and were calculated as: (N/EH) x 200,000, where
N = number of injuries and illnesses
EH = total hours worked by all employees during the calendar year
200,000 = base for 100 equivalent full-time workers (working 40 hours per week, 50 weeks per year)
NOTE: Dash indicates data do not meet publication guidelines.
SOURCE: Bureau of Labor Statistics, U.S. Department of Labor October 2009

1. As an occupational health specialist, you are reviewing trends in worker safety. Which of the following can you conclude based on the information in the table?

   A   Smelting and alloying of aluminum is the most dangerous job.

   B   Fewer police officers were injured in 2008 than firefighters.

   C   Some occupations are getting safer.

   D   There were no firefighters injured in 2007.

2. Based on the information in the table, what can you determine about the number of injuries in sports and skiing industries between 2007 and 2008?

   F   They increased.

   G   They decreased.

   H   They stayed the same.

   J   They can't be determined.

Write for Work

Suppose you work in one of the industries in the table on page 34. Choose an industry and write a memorandum to your manager in a notebook. Urge him or her to promote safety awareness in the workplace. Use the statistics in the table and three additional valid reasons or examples to support your position.

  Reading Extension

Turn to "Bomb Squad: No False Moves" on page 17 of *Reading Basics Advanced Reader*. After you have read and/or listened to the article, answer the questions below.

Circle the letter of the answer to each question.

1. Based on the article, what conclusion can you draw about how the Internet affects the bomb squad?

   A The Internet allows terrorists to share bomb-making techniques, so most IEDs are constructed in the same way and are easier to disarm.

   B The Internet allows the squad to track terrorists and find out where bombs might be planted.

   C The Internet allows terrorists to teach each other new methods of making IEDs, so it makes the bomb squad's work harder.

   D The Internet does not affect the bomb squad.

2. What can you conclude about how the use of robots affects the bomb squad's safety?

   F Robots make the work safer than walking up to the bomb and disarming it, but it is still very dangerous.

   G The robots eliminate any danger for the members of the squad.

   H The robots are rarely used because the bombs get stuck in their arms, which makes the work more dangerous.

   J The robots do not affect the bomb squad's safety.

Write the answer to each question.

3. What conclusions can you draw about why terrorists use IEDs rather than mass-produced bombs?

   _____

   _____

4. The author of the article writes, "With all the carnage these hidden bombs cause to soldiers and civilians, defusing them is one of the most important jobs in a war zone." Based on the rest of the article, is this a valid conclusion? Why or why not?

   _____

   _____

   _____

Explore Words

PREFIXES

A prefix is a word part that can be added to the beginning of many words. Prefixes have meaning, and adding a prefix changes the meaning of the word to which it is added. Here are some common prefixes, their meanings, and examples:

de-	"the opposite of"	*decaffeinated* (the opposite of caffeinated)
inter-	"between" or "among"	*interstate* (between states)
re-	"again"	*rearrange* (arrange again)
sub-	"below" or "less than"	*subnormal* (less than normal)

Read each phrase. Using a prefix from above, write a word with the same meaning as the phrase. Then use the word in a brief sentence.

1. marry again _____

2. less than standard _____

3. the opposite of activate _____

4. mix among _____

LATIN ROOTS

Many English words have Latin roots. Knowing the meanings of roots helps you figure out the meanings of unfamiliar words. Read these common Latin roots, what they mean, and the example words.

dict	"say"	*predict* (say before)
spect	"look"	*spectator* (a person who looks or watches)
ject	"throw"	*project* (throw forward)

Write one word that includes each Latin root above. Write a definition from the dictionary.

1. _____

Dictionary definition: _____

2. _____

Dictionary definition: _____

3. _____

Dictionary definition: _____

SYNONYMS

Synonyms are words that have the same or almost the same meanings. For example, *luscious* and *delectable* are synonyms.

Match each numbered word with its lettered synonym in the column on the right. Write the letter of the synonym on the line.

1. _____ despise   **a.** common   9. _____ enlarge   **a.** sufficient

2. _____ isolated   **b.** commotion   10. _____ grasp   **b.** consider

3. _____ ordinary   **c.** solitary   11. _____ spectator   **c.** flaw

4. _____ tumult   **d.** loathe   12. _____ adequate   **d.** magnify

5. _____ alter   **e.** jubilant   13. _____ discussion   **e.** stop

6. _____ euphoric   **f.** petty   14. _____ ponder   **f.** clutch

7. _____ treatment   **g.** transform   15. _____ weakness   **g.** conversation

8. _____ insignificant   **h.** remedy   16. _____ cease   **h.** viewer

ACADEMIC VOCABULARY

Knowing these high-frequency words will help you in many school subjects.

conclusion   a decision based on facts and knowledge

draw   to obtain something from

general   not specialized

currency   a system of money

grant   to give or allow something

Complete the sentences below using one of the words above.

1. Umberto looked at all the facts before he came to a _____.

2. Japera had a _____ feeling of uneasiness.

3. Lisha wanted to _____ cash out of the bank before she went on vacation.

4. The mayor refused to _____ the petitioner's request.

5. In the United States the _____ is both paper and coin.

Lesson 1.4

Summarize and Paraphrase

Summarizing and paraphrasing are useful skills for note-taking as well as for understanding and remembering what you read. When you summarize, you state the most important ideas and details in a passage as briefly as possible. You can combine important details and state them generally. A summary is much shorter than the original passage. A paraphrase may be the same length as the original. It includes all the details, but you state them in your own words. Read the example:

> Benjamin Franklin had unusual views on many subjects. From his own observations and experience, he developed a theory about catching a cold that closely matches modern medical facts. He was an avid outdoorsman and swimmer who found that chilly temperatures and cold water had no adverse effects on his body. After ruling out coldness and dampness as causes of colds, Franklin noticed that people often caught a cold after being in a crowded space. From that he deduced that colds were somehow passed from person to person when people were close to each other.

A good summary of this passage might be this: *Benjamin Franklin developed a theory that colds were caused by contact with other people, not through exposure to cold and wet weather.* Notice that the summary is much shorter than the original but states its main ideas.

A good paraphrase of the last two sentences of the passage might be this: *Franklin observed that being cold and wet did not cause colds. He concluded from his observations that people passed colds to one another when they were close together in a crowd.* Notice that the paraphrase fully explains all the sentences' details but uses different words than the original passage.

Write a summary of the passage below. Then write a paraphrase of the definition of machines in the second and third sentences.

> We live in the machine age. A machine is a device that has an arrangement of fixed and moving parts for doing work, each part having some special function. Machines make physical tasks easier by replacing or augmenting the energy that people expend. For instance, when you drive a screw into a piece of wood, you use your own effort to operate the screwdriver, but the screwdriver makes more effective use of that energy.

Summary: We live surrounded by machines that make it easier for us to accomplish physical tasks.

Paraphrase: A machine is a device with moving and stationary parts. A machine makes physical work easier by adding to or replacing people's energy.

Read each passage. Then write a summary. After reading the second passage, also write a paraphrase of the last three sentences.

Sometimes advertisements are hard to spot because they are presented in many forms. The sign above a supermarket, for example, simply identifies the store, but when the store illuminates the sign to draw attention to itself, it is advertising. In the early days of radio and TV, announcers would often interrupt programs and launch into commercials, so programming and advertising ran together with no interruption. Today, regulations try to separate the two, but sometimes it is difficult. For instance, is a music video entertainment or a commercial for a recording?

Summary

1. _____

_____

_____

The cinema has never been more popular than in the years immediately following World War II. In the United States, millions of people flocked to the theater to see the films that poured endlessly out of Hollywood studios. However, the rise of television soon provided stiff competition for the movie industry. In an effort to attract audiences, Hollywood started making fewer but more spectacular movies. The 1950s gave birth to a series of epic films, such as *Ben Hur*. Those star-studded movies were shot on location, filmed in "living color," and took years to make.

Summary

2. _____

_____

_____

Paraphrase of the last three sentences

3. _____

_____

_____

Read each passage. Then write a paraphrase of each passage.

> The Great Salt Lake in Utah is the largest inland body of salt water in the Western Hemisphere. The lake is called the Great Salt Lake because it has three to five times more salt content than the ocean.

1. _____

_____

_____

> Improving memory is an interest of many people. In the words of British author Thomas De Quincey, "It is notorious that the memory strengthens as you lay burdens upon it, and becomes trustworthy as you trust it."

2. _____

_____

_____

_____

Read the passage. Then write a summary of the passage.

> The first reported deaths from hailstones in the United States occurred in South Carolina, on May 8, 1784. The *South Carolina Gazette* described the storm as "a most extraordinary shower of hail, attended with thunder and lightning" and reported hailstones nine inches in circumference. The storm killed several people and many animals. It stripped leaves off trees, and it damaged grass.

3. _____

_____

_____

_____

Read each passage. Then circle the letter of the answer to each question.

> Because sponges remain in one place and grow slowly, people once thought they were not alive. Inside their hollow bodies, attached to special cells, are tail-like structures that move to create a current inside the sponge. As water moves through its body, the sponge filters out tiny food particles.

1. Choose the best paraphrase of the passage.

   A Sponges were once thought to be dead because they move so slowly. They have special tails that filter food from the water.

   B Sponges have a special way of filtering food from the water. People once didn't know they were alive because they grow so slowly.

   C People once did not know that sponges were alive because they grow so slowly. Sponges have a structure that resembles a tail attached to special cells in their bodies. They move the "tail" to create a current and filter food from the water.

   D People used to think sponges were not living things. Sponges don't move much, and they grow slowly. They have a special tail-like structure that moves water through their bodies.

2. Choose the best summary of the passage.

   F Sponges are living things that grow slowly and use a special tail to eat.

   G Sponges have hollow bodies and tails that moves water through their bodies.

   H Food particles pass through a sponge's body, and they get filtered by the sponge's tail.

   J Sponges are hollow and grow very slowly.

> Early American settlers and pioneers did not have time for idle play, so when they wanted to enjoy themselves, they would turn their work into fun. They made many of their necessary chores into group activities. These included logrollings, cornhuskings, quilting bees, and barn-raisings.

3. Choose the best summary of the passage.

   A Early American settlers and pioneers rarely played or had fun.

   B Group activities such as logrollings, cornhuskings, quilting bees, and barn-raisings were invented by early American settlers and pioneers.

   C Early American settlers did not like to enjoy themselves, so they spent all their time at cornhuskings, quilting bees, and barn-raisings.

   D Because early American settlers did not have much time for play, they often made their work into enjoyable group activities.

Workplace Skill: Summarize and Paraphrase a Purpose Statement

A purpose statement is a summary of the specific topic and goals of a longer, more detailed document. It is usually placed at the very beginning of the document. You will often need to summarize and paraphrase business documents. You may need to give the information to a coworker or retell the information to yourself to make sure you understand it.

Read the purpose statement. Then circle the letter of the answer to each question.

Process-improvement Plan
Purpose Statement

This document describes the process-improvement plan in the USA Jeans Customer Service Department. This plan lists process-improvement goals and outlines milestones for achieving them. This includes delegating responsibility, setting aside funds to achieve the goals, and comparing actual performance in relation to the goals.

The aim of this process-improvement plan is to lower department costs and to increase productivity and accuracy. This plan outlines the process-improvement strategy. It should be the basis for all department improvement activities.

This plan serves as the guideline for managers as they assign goals to their individual teams. This process-improvement plan will be updated at each of the four quarterly meetings to reflect ongoing department goals and responsibilities.

1. Which is the best summary of the purpose statement?

   A The process-improvement plan is designed to improve overall department performance.

   B The process-improvement plan will be updated quarterly.

   C Managers are the employees most affected by the process-improvement plan.

   D It is necessary to set aside funds to achieve the goals in the process-improvement plan.

2. What is the best paraphrase of the first sentence in the second paragraph?

   F The main aim of the plan is to lower department costs.

   G The plan's aims are to lower costs as well as increase productivity and accuracy.

   H Increased production will be the outcome of the plan.

   J The company wants employees to be accurate and productive.

Write the answer to the question.

3. Based on the purpose statement, what can you expect to find in the Process-improvement Plan?

_____

Write for Work

You are a team leader in the Customer Service Department of USA Jeans. In a notebook, write an e-mail to your team members explaining the reasons for the new department process-improvement plan. In two or three sentences, briefly summarize the goals of the process-improvement plan and how they will be implemented.

  Reading Extension

Turn to "Tornado Chasers: Eyes of the Storm" on page 25 of *Reading Basics Advanced Reader*. After you have read and/or listened to the article, answer the questions below.

Circle the letter of the answer to each question.

1. Which is the best summary of paragraph 2?

   A   Tornados can carry a motel sign for 30 miles, and they kill about 80 people each year.

   B   Tornados have winds of more than 250 miles per hour, which is twice as fast as the winds of some hurricanes.

   C   A tornado can destroy an entire neighborhood.

   D   A tornado is a very destructive storm that is characterized by high winds and occurs about 800 times in the United States every year.

2. Which is the best summary of paragraph 7?

   F   The *Dominator* is a heavy-duty truck that can drive into a tornado with winds under 150 miles per hour.

   G   The *Dominator* has bulletproof windows covering the regular windows to prevent them from being shattered.

   H   The *Dominator* has an outer shell made of steel.

   J   High winds are able to flip the *Dominator*.

Write the answer to each question.

3. Reread paragraph 1. Paraphrase the reasons that people become tornado chasers.

   _____

   _____

4. Reread paragraph 4. Write a summary of Faidley's accomplishments.

   _____

   _____

Explore Words

SPELLING: THE LETTERS f, ph, gh, ch

Many spellings can stand for the same sound. For example, the letter *f* stands for the sound you hear at the beginning of *finish*. That same sound is represented by the letters *ph* in *phone* and *elephant* and the letters *gh* in *laugh* and *cough*. On the other hand, the same spelling can stand for different sounds. For example, the letters *ch* stand for the sound you hear at the beginning of *cheese*. The same letters also sound like the letter *k* in *character* and like the letters *sh* in *machine*.

Say the words below. Underline the word in each row that contains the same sound as the underlined spelling in the first word. Circle the letter or letters that stand for the sound.

1. ne<u>ph</u>ew	people	naptime	fantastic	typical
2. re<u>f</u>use	trailer	tonsils	tougher	shoes
3. <u>k</u>itchen	matches	children	fences	stomach
4. enou<u>gh</u>	triumph	octopus	pumpkin	pneumonia
5. blea<u>ch</u>ers	scheme	chorus	charade	chocolate

GREEK ROOTS

Many English words have Greek roots. Greek roots have meanings. Knowing the meanings of roots can help you figure out the meanings of unfamiliar words. Read these common Greek roots, what they mean, and the example words.

tele "far"	+	*scope* "see"	*telescope* (a device for seeing far)
auto "self"	+	*graph* "write"	*autograph* (write your name)
bio "life"	+	*ology* "study of"	*biology* (the study of life)

Use your knowledge of Greek roots to figure out the meaning of each word. Write a short definition. Check your definition in a dictionary.

1. microscopic _____

2. biography _____

3. graphology _____

4. autopilot _____

5. telecommute _____

SPELLING: WORD ENDINGS

You can add the endings *-ed*, *-ing*, *-er*, and *-est* to the end of many words. When you add these endings to words that end with *-y*, some spelling rules apply:

- To add *-ed*, *-er*, or *-est* to a word that ends in a consonant and *-y*, change the *y* to *i*. Then add the ending: *skinny/skinnier/skinniest; hurry/hurried*.
- To add *-ing* to a word that ends in a consonant and *-y*, just add *-ing*: *hurry/hurrying; marry/marrying*.
- To add *-ed*, *-er*, *-est*, or *-ing* to a word that ends in a vowel and *-y*, just add the ending: *stay/stayed/staying; gray/grayer/grayest*.

Add the ending to each word. Write the new word on the line.

1. sunny + er _____

2. survey + ed _____

3. study + ing _____

4. fancy + est _____

5. envy + ing _____

6. beautify + ed _____

7. deny + ing _____

8. apply + ed _____

9. revive + ing _____

10. enjoy + ed _____

11. play + ing _____

12. worry + er _____

ACADEMIC VOCABULARY

Knowing these high-frequency words will help you in many school subjects.

summarize   to give a brief explanation of the main points

paraphrase   to restate in your own words

device   a thing made for a particular purpose

observe   to notice or perceive

conclude   to arrive at a judgment

Complete the sentences below using one of the words above.

1. Dominga made a _____ for turning the pages of her sheet music.

2. Chi had to _____ the plot of the long movie for her friend.

3. The researcher had to _____ the development of the mold cultures each day.

4. Keisha couldn't remember the exact quote, but she could _____ it.

5. The lawyer hoped that the judge would _____ that his client's e-mail was not admissible evidence.

Lesson 1.5

Identify Cause and Effect

INTRODUCE

One effective way to explain a topic is to state the reason something happens. A factor that makes something happen is a cause. A result of one or more causes is an effect.

Identifying cause-and-effect relationships is an important skill for understanding what you read. Sometimes writers use the words *cause* and *effect* to highlight the relationship between events in an obvious way. Other words and phrases that indicate cause-and-effect relationships are *so, therefore, since,* and *as a result*. Often, though, the writer will imply the cause-and-effect relationship and will not state it directly. You will have to identify the relationship by asking yourself questions like these: What has happened? What is the cause? What is the effect? Is there a direct relationship between them?

Sometimes a cause may be complicated or difficult to identify; additionally, many events have multiple causes. For example, imagine a person who slips and falls on an icy sidewalk. One cause might be the slipperiness of the ice, and another cause might be that the person was wearing the wrong kind of shoes. A third cause might be that the person was not looking where he or she was stepping. Read the example:

> The change of seasons occurs because of Earth's revolution around the sun and the tilt of Earth's axis.

There are two causes: Earth's revolution around the sun and the tilt of Earth's axis. There is one effect: the change of season. The key word *because* can help you identify the cause-and-effect relationship in the sentence.

Likewise, some causes have multiple effects. For example, the introduction of a new technology can lead to greater productivity for some companies, so one effect of the new technology is positive. On the other hand, the new technology might allow machines to do much of the work that people had previously done. This could mean that workers in many industries will lose their jobs, which is a negative effect.

Read the passage. Identify one cause and one effect in the passage.

> The British government passed many new laws taxing the colonists. As a result, colonists boycotted British goods to avoid paying these new taxes.

Cause: The British government passed new tax laws.

Effect: Colonists boycotted British goods.

The phrase *as a result* helps identify the cause-and-effect relationship in the sentences.

Read each passage. If a cause is stated below the passage, write the effect. If an effect is stated below the passage, write the cause.

The first building to be called a skyscraper was built in Chicago, Illinois, between 1884 and 1885. The Home Insurance Company had the building constructed on LaSalle and Adams Streets in the Windy City. It was designed by an architect named William Le Baron Jenney. Because the walls could not bear the weight of the building, a steel frame performed that function.

1. Cause: A steel frame was constructed for the first skyscraper.

Effect: _____

Space probes to Venus have photographed structures that might be the remains of coastlines. For this and other reasons, scientists think that Venus may have had oceans and an atmosphere at one time. Life may have existed there, but the rising levels of carbon dioxide caused the greenhouse effect to increase dramatically. The surface temperatures increased to 467°C (862°F), where they remain today. If any water had once gathered on Venus, it boiled away a very long time ago.

2. Cause: Space probes have photographed structures that might be the remains of coastlines.

Effect: _____

3. Cause: _____

Effect: Temperatures on Venus increased.

Have you ever wondered why the capital of the United States is not in any of the 50 states? When the 13 original colonies formed a union after the American Revolution, men and women from every colony wanted to house the capital in their home territory. To solve this problem, the founders decided to put the capital in a location not affiliated with any particular state. In 1791 George Washington picked the site for the capital. He chose the 68-square-mile area now known as the District of Columbia.

4. Cause: _____

Effect: The U.S. capital is not housed in any state.

Read the passage. Then fill in the graphic organizer with the cause or effect.

You can think of atoms as seekers. They seek to become more stable by gaining, losing, or sharing electrons, which is why they form chemical bonds. Sometimes a bond breaks, and this changes a stable atom or molecule into two unstable units called free radicals. Free radicals seek to regain stability by "stealing" an electron from another atom or molecule. This, in turn, changes the "victim" into a free radical. In the human body, uncontrolled free radicals can damage cells and tissues. Compounds called antioxidants, found in many fruits and vegetables, donate electrons and, therefore, neutralize free radicals.

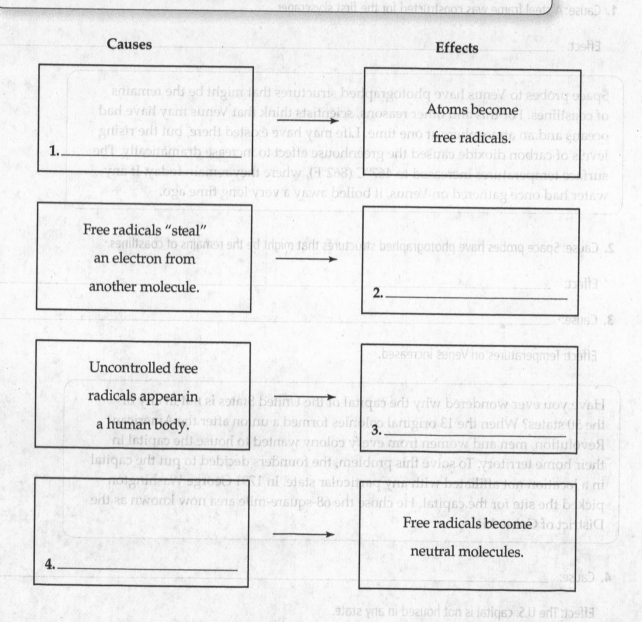

Causes   Effects

1. _____

Atoms become
free radicals.

Free radicals "steal"
an electron from
another molecule. →

2. _____

Uncontrolled free
radicals appear in
a human body. →

3. _____

4. _____ →

Free radicals become
neutral molecules.

Read each passage. Then circle the letter of the answer to each question.

Antarctica, located at the South Pole, is covered by ice sheets that are thousands of feet thick. Over the years many different countries have sent expeditions to explore this area. Early expeditions investigated the potential for whaling in the region, but later expeditions have focused on other things. Since 1945 Antarctica has experienced a warming trend. Huge ice shelves have disintegrated or collapsed, and penguin populations have declined.

1. What is the most reasonable cause for the loss of ice shelves in the Antarctic?

A numerous expeditions sent to explore the region

B warming trends

C lack of snowfall

D ice shelves breaking off

2. What is the most reasonable cause for the decline of penguin populations?

F They have been over-hunted.

G They are prey for whales.

H Whaling has reduced their food supply.

J Warmer temperatures have caused loss of habitats.

As people grow older, they need to exercise more. People tend to gain weight with age, as their basal metabolic rate, or the rate at which they burn calories, decreases. An older person's appetite may not decrease, but that person no longer needs as many calories as he or she did in earlier years. Many older people also exercise less than they did when they were young, so they burn fewer calories.

3. What is one cause for people gaining weight as they grow older?

A Their metabolic rate increases as they age.

B Their appetites increase as they age.

C Their metabolic rate decreases as they age.

D They exercise more as they age.

4. If an older person continues to eat as many calories as when he or she was younger, what will the effect be?

F The person does not need as many calories as he or she used to.

G The person will exercise less as he or she grows older.

H The person will lose weight.

J The person will gain weight.

Workplace Skill:
Identify Cause and Effect by Reading an Instrument Gauge

In the workplace, you often need to use graphics to find information. The airspeed indicator is an instrument guage that is located in the cockpit of an airplane. It is color-coded to give the pilot the information he or she needs to safely fly the plane. The markings show speeds (in miles per hour) at which it is safe to perform various functions as well as speeds that the pilot should not go over due to the risks of damage to the plane.

Read the instrument gauge. Use the information in the graphic and your own knowledge to answer the questions. Then circle the letter of the answer to each question.

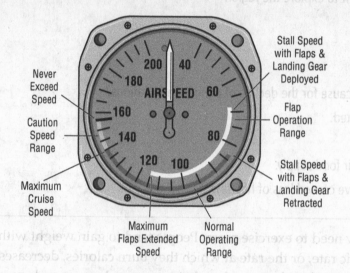

1. Which could be an effect of flying at 130 miles per hour?

   A   The landing gear will deploy.

   B   You will be at maximum cruise speed.

   C   Your flaps may be damaged if they are extended.

   D   You are below the normal operating range.

2. If you are a pilot, what is the minimum speed you should be going if your landing gear is deployed?

   F   70 mph

   G   80 mph

   H   100 mph

   J   120 mph

3. Which could be an effect of flying at 150 miles per hour?

   A   You run the risk of stalling.

   B   You will be able to extend the flaps.

   C   You will have exceeded maximum cruise speed.

   D   Your landing gear will deploy.

4. What might have caused the manufacturer to include ranges marked *caution speed* or *never exceed*?

   F   They want the pilots to fly in the caution range.

   G   They want the pilots to be warned if they are getting too close to top speed.

   H   They want to use extra colors on the instrument.

   J   They want to be able to fly at top speed.

Write for Work

Imagine that you are a flight instructor training a new pilot. In a notebook, create a page for a training manual that explains what the airspeed indicator is and why it is important for a pilot to pay attention to it at all times. Refer to the diagram on page 50. Use specific speeds and details from the airspeed indicator in your explanation.

 Reading Extension

Turn to "High-rise Window Washers: A Bird's-eye View" on page 33 of *Reading Basics Advanced Reader*. After you have read and/or listened to the article, answer the questions below.

Circle the letter of the answer to each question.

1. What caused Estrada and Gonzalez's platform to plunge sharply downward?

   A Estrada and Gonzalez pushed the wrong button.

   B There were very high winds that day.

   C One of the platform supports started to collapse.

   D The building had many broken windows.

2. Which was NOT a result of Estrada and Gonzalez's ordeal?

   F The men quit their jobs.

   G The men suffered minor injuries.

   H The men sued the building owner.

   J Two dozen windows shattered.

3. What was the cause of Robert Domaszowec's fall?

   A The new windows were not installed correctly.

   B Domaszowec leaned too far away from the building.

   C Domaszowec was very overweight.

   D Domaszowec was inexperienced.

Write the answer to each question.

4. What might have resulted from the police investigation of Domaszowec's death?

_____

5. What is one result of a window washer going higher "up the ladder"?

_____

Explore Words

SUFFIXES -ive, -ic, -ish

A suffix is a word part that can be added to the end of many words. Adding a suffix changes the meaning of a base word. For example, the suffixes -ive and -ic mean "pertains to" or "tends to." So, *attractive* means "tends to attract," and *caloric* means "pertaining to calories." The suffix -ish means "like," so *childish* means "like a child."

Read each phrase. Using a suffix from above, write a word with the same meaning as the phrase. Then write a brief sentence using the new word.

1. like a fool _____

_____

2. pertains to heroes _____

_____

3. tends to create _____

_____

SPELLING: HOMOPHONES

Homophones are words that sound alike but are spelled differently and have different meanings. For example, *horse* and *hoarse* are homophones.

Complete each sentence with a homophone. Write the word on the line.

1. I wanted to buy that used car, but I lost the phone number of the _____. (cellar, seller)

2. My dream is to live on a tropical _____. (aisle, isle)

3. A two-_____ diamond is huge! (carat, carrot)

4. Her kids are not _____ to watch TV after school. (aloud, allowed)

5. Smoking is _____ in most public buildings. (band, banned)

6. Our _____ pays us 300 dollars per month. (boarder, border)

7. What is the _____ number on the box? (cereal, serial)

8. Please don't _____ in my life! (meddle, medal)

9. Nizhoni went to the store to buy a new pair of _____. (genes, jeans)

Reading Basics · Advanced

Some words have more than one meaning. For example, *season* means "to add flavorings to food." A season is also one of four periods in a year. You can use context clues—other words in the same or nearby sentences—to figure out which meaning is intended.

Use context clues in each sentence that help you know the intended meaning of the underlined word. Circle the letter of the intended meaning.

1. Which <u>volume</u> of the encyclopedia are you using?
   a. a book
   b. the loudness of sound

2. I don't think the injury <u>warrants</u> a trip to the emergency room.
   a. justifies or deserves
   b. written orders or documents

3. The mayor spoke with <u>conviction</u> about her plan to reduce crime.
   a. the process of proving guilt
   b. a strong belief

4. Was that <u>deliberate</u> or an accident?
   a. intentional
   b. to consider something carefully

5. Friends <u>console</u> each other during difficult times.
   a. be a source of comfort
   b. a small cabinet

6. The ore in the <u>mine</u> was very valuable.
   a. belonging to me
   b. a pit in the ground for extracting minerals

Knowing these high-frequency words will help you in many school subjects.

cause	something that produces an effect
effect	a result or consequence
likewise	in a similar manner
identify	to recognize or point out
obvious	easily seen, recognized, or understood

Complete the sentences below using one of the words above.

1. One _____ of the traffic jam is that I am now late for dinner.

2. Asmera was able to _____ her missing bag to claim it from the lost and found.

3. The doctor still had not determined the _____ of the outbreak.

4. It was _____ that the two had romantic feelings for each other.

5. Paulo will write a letter from his vacation, and _____, Marietta will send a postcard.

Lesson 1.6

Understand Author's Purpose

Everything you read is written for a reason. The reason for writing is called the author's purpose, and the basic purposes are to persuade, to inform, to explain, to entertain, or to describe. Identifying the author's purpose will help you better understand the meaning of the passage. If the author's purpose is to persuade, he or she might present only one side of an argument or only give a few facts in order to convince you to think the way he or she does. When the author's purpose is to inform, the author gives information about a subject or teaches something. When the purpose is to explain, the author might give instructions for how to do something or give details showing why something happens. If the author's purpose is to entertain, you may find that the writing is funny, interesting, or suspenseful. When the purpose is to describe, the author creates a picture using words.

An author may have more than one purpose. For example, a persuasive article can also be entertaining, and an entertaining article can also be informative. However, most writers have a primary purpose, and that purpose is usually apparent. Read the example and think about what the author's primary purpose is.

> Every child should hear a story before being put to bed each night. While an adult reads a bedtime story to a child, the child has a chance to quiet down and get ready for sleep. Being close to an adult he or she loves gives the child a sense of contentment. Finally, bedtime stories can start the child on a lifelong love of reading.

The primary purpose is to persuade. The word *should* in the first sentence signals that the statement is an opinion. Details are provided to support this opinion.

Read the following passage and identify the author's purpose.

> Have you met your neighbors yet? They are not very sociable, but on a clear night you can glimpse them in the sky. Mars is sometimes as close as 55 million kilometers from your front door. It has a rocky, lifeless surface and a thin, oxygen-free atmosphere. Your other neighbor, Venus, has a thick atmosphere that would crush you instantly if your blood did not boil first. If you are invited for coffee on either planet, think twice before accepting.

This passage describes Mars and Venus, the two planets closest to Earth. The author presents information about both planets in a humorous way, and you can infer that the author's purpose is to entertain. You could also argue that the author's main purpose is to inform, and that he or she uses humor to help relate the information.

Read each passage. Then write whether the author's main purpose is to inform, persuade, describe, explain, or entertain.

> Only the sound of our boots scraping against rock and loose pebbles broke the silence as we moved deeper into the cave. Breathing had become an effort. The air, long stagnant from being kept in this tomblike cave, burned our throats and left a rancid taste. Foul-smelling and heavy, it seemed to stick in our lungs after each intake of breath. The miner's lamps on our helmets cut a thin slice out of the thick, black gloom around us.

1. Purpose: _____

> Cartoonist Al Hirschfeld hid his daughter's name in his famous caricatures for decades. Finding the name "Nina" was something of a sport for Hirschfeld fans. Next to the artist's signature was a number telling how many times he had skillfully woven Nina's name into the cartoon.

2. Purpose: _____

> On your next visit to the supermarket, count the product labels that include the word *natural*. You will find it in phrases such as "all natural ingredients" and "natural goodness," but what does *natural* mean? Many poisons are natural, and so are wood, rocks, and other things people cannot eat. Words such as *natural* are often used to sell products, not to provide facts about them.

3. Purpose: _____

> Your heart rate tells you how many beats your heart is beating per minute and can vary depending on your activities. To find your heart rate, you first need to find your pulse by lightly pressing on your skin either on the inside of your wrist or the side of your neck. When you feel a small beat below your skin, you've found your pulse. In a span of 6 seconds, count how many beats you feel. Then, multiply that number by 10 and you have your heart rate.

4. Purpose: _____

Read the passages. Then circle the letter of the answer to each question.

Passage 1

The approaching night in the jungle was, in itself, a threat. As the night deepened, an eerie silence enveloped the thatched village, and the people themselves were quiet. Tethered cattle stood quietly, roosting chickens did not stir, and wise goats made no noise. Thus it had been for countless centuries, and thus it would continue to be. The people of the village knew the jungle. They had trodden its dim paths, forded its sulky rivers, borne its steaming heat, and were familiar with its deer, crocodiles, screaming green parrots, and countless other creatures.

Passage 2

The Portuguese explorer Ferdinand Magellan should be known as the greatest navigator of all time. The fleet under his command discovered the Strait of Magellan, a passageway at the tip of South America that connects the Atlantic and Pacific oceans. Although he died before his voyage was completed, his navigational planning helped his crew finish their trip around the world. Magellan's discovery of the Strait of Magellan helped other explorers learn more about the Pacific Ocean. The most important result was that his long voyage proved that the world is actually round.

Passage 3

Over the centuries, church bells did more than just beckon people to services. During the Middle Ages, for instance, they had several practical civic uses. Bells announced the evening curfew, warned people of fire, and reminded citizens of tax deadlines. Some people believed that the metallic bells had the power to scare off ghosts and demons.

---

1. Which passage uses facts to persuade the audience?

   A   passage 1

   B   passage 2

   C   passage 3

   D   none of the above

2. Which passage's main purpose is to inform?

   F   passage 1

   G   passage 2

   H   passage 3

   J   all of the above

3. Which passage uses vivid detail for the main purpose of describing?

   A   passage 1

   B   passage 2

   C   passage 3

   D   none of the above

4. Which could be a secondary purpose of passage 2?

   F   to inform

   G   to persuade

   H   to instruct

   J   none of the above

Read each passage. Then circle the letter of the answer to each question.

You have probably been warned not to stand under a tree during an electrical storm. That is excellent advice because one lightning bolt can send millions of volts of electricity directly underneath the bark. When that happens, the sap immediately heats to the boiling point, which causes a violent expulsion of steam to rip through the bark. Large chunks of the tree are often catapulted outward. This is a dangerous possible consequence of using a tree for shelter: a flying chunk of wood can be deadly. If you are caught by a storm while hiking in the woods, do not stand under the trees.

1. What is the author's main purpose in the passage?

   A   to persuade

   B   to entertain

   C   to describe

   D   to explain

2. Which of the following does the author use to achieve his or her purpose?

   F   lists of facts and statistics

   G   cause-and-effect explanation

   H   humor

   J   detailed instructions

Somewhere out in the ocean is a great mass of moving blubber—a blue whale. Many people think it is the mightiest animal that has ever lived, but this giant beast with a giant mouth has no teeth. Instead, it has hundreds of thin plates. Its stomach is huge, capable of holding one ton of krill at a time. This beast can weigh up to 200 tons, but it survives by eating krill, an animal less than six inches long.

3. What is the author's main purpose in the passage?

   A   to persuade

   B   to describe

   C   to entertain

   D   to explain

4. Which of the following does the author use to achieve his or her purpose?

   F   summary

   G   humor

   H   step-by-step instructions

   J   specific, vivid details

Workplace Skill:
Understand Author's Purpose in a Memo

Employers use memos (short for memorandums) to give information about their company plans and policies. They also use memos to describe company procedures. Sometimes they use memos to persuade employees to act in a certain way. To identify the author's purpose for writing the memo, ask yourself what the author wants you to think, do, or feel as a result of reading it.

Read the memo. Then circle the letter of the answer to each question below the box.

Memorandum

To: Eduardo Hernandez, Director of Marketing
From: Odion Carter, Market Research Coordinator
Date: May 22
Subject: Choconana Cereal Launch

Market research has shown that our current product launch for Choconana cereal needs to be revised. Our target audience for this cereal is kids between the ages of 8 and 12. This age group no longer watches morning or afternoon cartoons. However, most use the Internet every day. They spend about six hours per week surfing the web and visiting social media sites. I strongly suggest that we shift our focus and funds from television advertising to Internet advertising. This will help us represent Choconana cereal as a relevant product for our core age group. It will also ensure that our target audience is exposed to the product and help establish the overall Great Grains cereal group as a youth-friendly brand.

Attachments: Focus Group Results, January–April
Survey Analysis, January–April

1. What is the author's main purpose for writing this memo?

   A to give information about kids' Internet use

   B to explain how to do a product launch

   C to convince the marketing department to revise the product launch

   D to persuade kids between the ages of 8 and 12 to buy cereal

2. What is a second reason the author wrote the memo?

   F to persuade the reader of the memo to think about surfing the Web more

   G to explain to the reader of the memo the reasons that kids do not watch cartoons

   H to inform the reader of the memo about trends in the market

   J to convince the reader of the memo that the brand name should be changed

Write for Work

Imagine that you are Eduardo Hernandez. In a notebook, write a response to Odion Carter's memo that shows that you understood the main purpose of his memo. Address his concerns and describe what changes you will make to the product launch.

Workplace Extension

Moving Up in the Workplace

Kelly Smith started her new job as a food service worker in a nursing home. She met Jimmy Daley, who was the supervisor in charge of training new workers. Jimmy showed Kelly how to set the cooked foods on the service line and how much food to place on the plates. Jimmy showed her how to use gloves so that her hands would not touch the food.

Within a few months, Kelly learned the names of the people who came through her line, and she greeted each with a smile. She loved working in the nursing home, but she wanted to do more. Kelly started to learn more about nutrition on her own. Kelly thought she might want to become a dietary technician or nutritionist. She knew that she would have to go to college and that it would be difficult, but she really wanted to move up to a higher position at the nursing home.

Circle the letter of the answer to each question.

1. What is one of the most useful steps Kelly can do at this point in her career?

    A   talk to one of the nursing home patients about the weekly menu

    B   speak to a dietary technician or nutritionist about the skills needed for the job

    C   talk to her friend Mindy about what job Mindy thinks is best

    D   tell her supervisor that she is unhappy and might leave

2. Kelly started to learn more about nutrition on her own. This shows you that she is

    F   unwilling to think and plan ahead.

    G   motivated and positive about her future career.

    H   concerned about losing her job.

    J   unhappy about what she is currently doing.

Write the answer to the question.

3. Imagine that you are Kelly Smith. What steps would you take to become a dietary technician or nutritionist?

_____

_____

Explore Words

SPELLING: CONTRACTIONS

A contraction is a short way to write two words. An apostrophe (') takes the place of the letters that are dropped when the contraction is formed. For example, the words *he is* become *he's*. The words *is not* become *isn't*.

Match each pair of words in the left column with the appropriate contraction in the right column. Write the letter on the line. Then write contractions from the list to complete the passage below.

_____	**1.** I have	**a.**	I'm
_____	**2.** I am	**b.**	can't
_____	**3.** there is	**c.**	didn't
_____	**4.** can not	**d.**	there's
_____	**5.** did not	**e.**	I've

I think (6) _____ nothing more enjoyable than planning a vacation, but I

(7) _____ decide where I want to go this year. (8) _____ thinking of

taking a biking trip. (9) _____ always wanted to try one. My friend Carmelita

went on a biking trip in California last year. She (10) _____ have any complaints!

SUFFIXES *-ance, -ant, -ent*

A suffix is a word part that can be added to the end of many words. A suffix often changes the part of speech of the word to which it is added. For example, *ignore* is a verb that means "to refuse to be aware." *Ignorance* is a noun that means "lack of knowledge or awareness," and *ignorant* is an adjective that means "lacking knowledge or awareness."

Choose a suffix to complete each word. Then write the suffix on the line.

Dear (1) Particip_____ (ant, ance),

We are pleased to invite you to join us. Your (2) attend_____ (ant, ance) will qualify

you to win one of ten (3) extravag_____ (ant, ance) prizes. Don't be (4) hesit_____

(ant, ance)! We are (5) confid_____ (ent, ence) that you will be glad you came. If you

need directions or other (6) assist_____ (ant, ance), please call. If the line is busy, be

(7) toler_____ (ant, ance) and try again later. See you on November 20!

Many words are made up of a base word or root plus a prefix and/or a suffix. Being able to break an unfamiliar word into its parts can help you read the word and can give you clues to its meaning.

Read each word. On the lines, write the prefix, the base word or root, and the suffix or word ending.

1. subjected

2. instructing

3. nonbeliever

4. unicyclist

5. international

6. disappearance

7. reformatted

8. misidentified

9. transporting

ACADEMIC VOCABULARY

Knowing these high-frequency words will help you in many school subjects.

purpose — the reason something is done

inform — to give facts or information

persuade — to convince someone to do or think something through reasoning

argument — a set of reasons given with the goal of persuading others

consequence — the effect of an action or circumstance

Complete the sentences below using one of the words above.

1. The _____ of the rally was to support the mayoral candidate.

2. The caller tried to _____ Po to vote yes on the proposition.

3. Jorge did not read the document, and as a _____, he was unprepared for the meeting.

4. I need to _____ the workers of the new safety regulation.

5. Even without looking closely, Bana could tell that there were many holes in the _____.

Lesson 1.7
Find the Main Idea

Almost everything you read has a main idea, which is the most important idea of the passage. The main idea can be stated or implied. Many readers believe that a stated main idea must appear in the first sentence of a passage, but this is not always the case. A stated main idea can appear anywhere within a passage. If the main idea is implied, it is communicated indirectly through supporting details. The reader must deduce the main idea by examining the information and deciding what links all the details together.

To find the main idea of a passage, ask yourself the following question: *What is the most important thing the writer is saying?* Then decide if a sentence in the passage contains the main idea. If no sentence contains the most important idea in the passage, the main idea is implied.

Read the example below in which the main idea is stated in the first sentence. All of the details that follow support and relate to it.

> The Mississippi River has always been important to the growth of the U.S. economy. The river has supplied water to the people and industries in nearby cities. Trading with the surrounding area has been made easier by using the river for transportation.

Now read the passage below in which the main idea is implied. The main idea of this passage could be that each part of the upper class in Egyptian society had a different role to play. This idea is not stated directly, but each sentence supports it.

> The pharaoh and other members of the royal family were at the top of Egyptian society, followed by the upper class of priests and nobles. Priests took care of the temples and celebrated religious ceremonies. Nobles oversaw the government.

Read the passage and decide whether it has a stated or implied main idea.

> (1) The United Nations (UN) is headed by a secretary-general. (2) The secretary-general is elected by the members of the UN General Assembly, which includes a representative from each member country. (3) The secretary-general serves for five years, and at the end of this time, he or she can be re-elected to another term. (4) There have been eight secretary-generals since the UN was established.

Sentence 1 makes a general statement about the leader of the United Nations, while sentences 2 through 4 provide details and examples about the office of the secretary-general. Only sentence 1 is general enough to include the ideas of the other sentences, so sentence 1 states the main idea.

Read each passage. If the main idea of the passage is directly stated, circle *stated*. Then write the stated main idea on the line. If the main idea of the passage is implied, circle *implied*. Then write the implied main idea on the line.

> Nerve cells are long and thin, and this enables them to send information from one part of the body to another. Red blood cells carry oxygen through the body, so these cells are in the form of a flattened disk that can flow through thin blood vessels. A sperm cell is a cell that travels to an egg cell. Each sperm cell has a tail that allows it to travel quickly.

1. stated   implied

_____

_____

> A formidable group of people sparked America's industrialization. Andrew Carnegie, John D. Rockefeller, J. P. Morgan, Cornelius Vanderbilt, and others put together the giant companies that ruled America's economy. Their collective power was often misused to keep prices high and wages low. These company owners got laws passed that were favorable to their businesses.

2. stated   implied

_____

_____

> As a library volunteer, you can replace books on the shelves or help organize the periodicals. You can also assist the staff at the circulation desk when there are long lines of people. When a person is having a difficult time finding a book or periodical in the stacks, you can help the person locate it. Because of all the recent budget cuts, the professional staff is much smaller these days. The librarians will be grateful for any help you can give.

3. stated   implied

_____

_____

Read each passage. State the main idea of each passage in your own words. Be sure it is not too broad or too narrow.

U.S. Postal Service mail carriers do not deliver mail only on foot or in a truck. In the early 1900s, some mail carriers used skis, snowshoes, and even mule trains to deliver the mail. Even today, some mail is dropped by parachute in parts of Alaska.

1. _____

_____

Kangaroos cannot run, yet even track stars wouldn't be able to keep up with them. A kangaroo's long, powerful hind legs are ideal for jumping. Kangaroos leap up to seven feet high to jump over hurdles or other obstructions. They go about 30 miles an hour, and their speed allows them to escape predators.

2. _____

_____

Most people know that the Pilgrims landed at Plymouth, Massachusetts, in 1620, but many people do not know that Plymouth was not the first place the *Mayflower* dropped anchor. The *Mayflower* first landed at Provincetown, at the tip of Cape Cod. Some of the Pilgrims stayed there while others scouted for a good place to settle.

3. _____

_____

Ecology is a branch of science that is concerned with the relationships among organisms and their environments. Ecology was brought to the attention of the public and the government of the United States in the early 1960s. That is when Rachel Carson published *Silent Spring*, a book in which she described how pesticides were destroying plant and animal life.

4. _____

_____

Read each passage. Then circle the letter of the answer that states the passage's main idea.

> The United Nations (UN) is an international organization. The land and building of the UN headquarters, while located in New York City, belong to all the member nations of the UN. In addition, the UN has its own postage stamps and police force. The United Nations has six official languages, which are Arabic, Chinese, English, French, Russian, and Spanish. The UN building includes many pieces of fine art, which were contributed by member nations.

1. A The UN is an international organization.

B The UN has its own postage stamps and police force.

C The UN has six official languages.

D The UN headquarters belongs to its member nations.

> Suppose that one of your best employees is not performing well. Instead of rushing to judge or criticize, consider the possibility that he or she has a problem. Set up a meeting in which you can express your concerns and listen to your employee's point of view. You may very well be able to solve the problem together. If you treat an unsatisfactory employee with compassion, honesty, and respect, you have a good chance of improving the situation.

2. F Suppose that one of your best employees is not performing well.

G You can often improve the poor performance of an employee by talking to the employee with respect and understanding.

H Set up a meeting in which you can express concerns and listen to an employee who is not performing well.

J You may be able to solve the problem together.

> (1) Once a mockingbird was living in a tree outside my brother's bedroom window. (2) From early morning to late at night, the bird loudly mimicked the songs of other birds. (3) With all that noise, it became nearly impossible for my brother to sleep, study, or even think. (4) Finally, he set up an audio recorder next to the window to record the mockingbird. (5) When he played back the recording, the confused bird started to mimic itself. (6) Soon the bird flew away, never to be heard from again. (7) My brother had found a clever solution to the problem of the noisy bird!

3. A sentence 1   **C** sentence 6

B sentence 3   **D** sentence 7

Workplace Skill: Find the Main Idea in a Memo about the Office Recycling Program

Most companies have established a recycling policy for the workplace to provide guidelines for employees and to protect the environment. To understand a company policy, you need to understand its main idea: the idea that links all its details.

Read the memo. Then circle the letter of the answer to each question below the box.

Memorandum

To: All employees
From: Maintenance
Date: April 5, 2011
Subject: Office recycling

Kantaka Engineering Office Recycling Program

Separate the paper recyclables from nonpaper recyclables. Large green containers are for paper recyclables. Tall blue containers are for nonpaper recyclables. The containers are located in the lunchroom and the copy/supply room. Every Friday, maintenance will collect all recyclables and bring them to the recycling center. The following items are recyclable in our program:

Mixed Paper White paper, envelopes, newsprint, colored paper, file folders, lined paper, computer paper, magazines, and shredded paper can be placed in the green containers.

Cardboard Cardboard should be flattened and placed in a conspicuous location, such as outside an office door or next to a regular trash can, for pickup by maintenance.

Bottles and Cans Please clean all bottles and cans and place them in the blue containers.

E-Waste Old/outdated electronics such as computers, monitors, and other peripherals (speakers, printers, etc.) contain heavy metals that if disposed of improperly (in a regular landfill) can be toxic to the environment and potentially the public. Call the Information Technology Department, and it will dispose of this type of material.

---

1. What is the main idea of the memo?

A Paper recyclables should be separated from nonpaper recyclables.

B Employees should recycle correctly.

C Cardboard recyclables should be handled differently from bottles and cans.

D The Information Technology Department is in charge of e-waste materials.

2. What is the main idea of the e-waste section?

F E-waste material should not be handled any differently than other recyclables.

G The Maintenance Department should dispose of all e-waste every Thursday.

H Employees should think about the environment whenever they dispose of any material.

J E-waste cannot be thrown out with regular trash and should be handled specially.

Write for Work

There are four main categories, or sections, in the memo on page 66. Each one describes a specific kind of material to recycle. Read each description. Then write the main idea of each of the four sections of the recycling program memo in a notebook.

Workplace Extension

Negotiating for a Raise

Juan Ramirez liked his job with the maintenance department at the Comfort Zone Hotel because the people he worked with were friendly and because his boss, Ms. Chan, seemed to like him. There was a problem, though, because Juan had been employed at the hotel for almost three years and had received only one pay raise. He thought he deserved another raise by now and kept waiting for his boss to bring it up. His friend Hoa said, "What are you waiting for? You should speak to Ms. Chan and bring the matter up yourself."

By the next morning, Juan had prepared two pages of notes. He had worked hard in the last year, and he made a list of his accomplishments. In addition to his normal job responsibilities, he had trained a new maintenance worker. He had also improved conditions in the hotel's maintenance supply room. He was rarely late for work and had called in sick only twice. Armed with his notes, he asked for a meeting with Ms. Chan.

Circle the letter of the answer to each question.

1. What is one strong point that Juan should make that could help him negotiate for a raise?

   A He has taken the time to write up two pages of notes on his accomplishments.

   B He felt that he deserved a raise.

   C He has gone beyond his job description in training a new maintenance worker.

   D He will leave if he does not get a raise.

2. What is the proper attitude to convey when asking for a raise?

   F respectful but confident

   G respectful but unhappy

   H confident and boastful

   J serious and sullen

Write the answer to the question.

3. Do you think Juan's friend Hoa gave him the right advice? Explain why or why not.

_____

_____

Explore Words

PREFIXES *uni-*, *bi-*, *tri-*

Some prefixes have meanings that indicate number. For example, the prefix *uni-* means "one," the prefix *bi-* means "two," and the prefix *tri-* means "three."

Read each definition. Then circle the letter of the word with that meaning.

1. a type of cycle with one wheel

   A bicycle

   B unicycle

   C tricycle

   D cyclotron

2. a set of three books

   F encyclopedia

   G trilogy

   H series

   J boxed set

3. an athletic competition consisting of three events

   A Olympics

   B unithlon

   C biathlon

   D triathlon

4. happening twice in a year

   F triannual

   G biannual

   H annual

   J preannual

5. bring parts together into one whole

   A unbreak

   B reform

   C fracture

   D unify

6. to cut into two pieces

   F unisect

   G bisect

   H trisect

   J insect

ANALOGIES

An analogy is a word sentence that describes a relationship between two pairs of words.
Analogies always include a colon (:) that stands for "is to." Read this analogy:

Cold : hot as *young : old.*

To complete an analogy, you need to figure out the relationship between the two words.
In the example, both pairs of words are antonyms; they have opposite meanings. Here are
two other common kinds of analogies:

- Grammatical: *Man : men* as *mouse : mice.* The first word in each pair is a singular
  noun. The second word in each pair is plural.

- Synonyms: *Thin : slender* as *fat : chubby.* Both pairs have almost the same meaning.

Select the word that best completes each analogy. Write the word on the line.

1. *Near : far* as *large* : _____. (*big, small*)

2. *Blue : blew* as *hoarse* : _____. (*horse, voice*)

3. *Puppy : dog* as *cub* : _____. (*kittens, bear*)

4. *Hired : fired* as *healthy* : _____. (*sick, happy*)

CONTEXT CLUES

Use context clues to help you figure out the meaning of an unfamiliar word. Look for clues in the same sentence as the unfamiliar word or in nearby sentences.

Read the passage. Use context clues to figure out the meanings of the underlined words. Circle the letter of the best meaning.

> Varied forms of entertainment became available to a wide public in the 1920s. The mass-produced automobile provided much of the middle class with a mobility never before known. Moviegoing became a favorite pastime. The advent of movies with soundtracks in the late 1920s made a visit to the cinema even more exciting.

1. As used in this passage, *mass-produced* means

   A "made in large quantities."

   B "invented."

   C "made in limited quantities."

   D "brand new."

2. As used in this passage *mobility* means

   F "vehicle."

   G "means of entertainment."

   H "ability to move about."

   J "wealth."

3. As used in this passage *pastime* means.

   A "meal."

   B "past history."

   C "time long ago."

   D "form of recreation."

4. As used in this passage *advent* means

   F "cost."

   G "arrival."

   H "end."

   J "popularity."

ACADEMIC VOCABULARY

Knowing these high-frequency words will help you in many school subjects.

deduce   to draw a logical conclusion

imply   to suggest

examine   to inspect or study closely

link   to form a connection between

establish   to set up something permanent

Complete the sentences below using one of the words above.

1. The workers at the museum couldn't wait to _____ the fossil.

2. The writer tried to _____ a relationship between the characters without stating it outright.

3. Nyah wrote an extra paragraph to _____ her introduction to the conclusion.

4. Based on the clues, Masika was able to _____ the solution to the mystery.

5. The Pilgrims were not the first to _____ a permanent colony in North America.

Unit 1 Review

Recognize and Recall Details

Details are words and phrases that give more information about a subject. They can be examples, descriptions, facts, or opinions. To find specific facts or details, you can scan passages by rereading a passage quickly but closely.

Understand Stated and Implied Concepts

Sometimes the ideas in a passage are clearly stated. Sometimes they are implied, and you need to use other information to make an inference. You may need to read a passage several times to understand all the stated and implied concepts presented.

Draw Conclusions

When you draw conclusions, you use several pieces of information to make a statement about people, places, events, or ideas. You draw a conclusion based on things that are stated directly, things that are implied, and things that you already know.

Summarize and Paraphrase

When you summarize, you state the most important ideas and details in a passage as briefly as possible. When you paraphrase, you restate a passage, including details, in your own words.

Identify Cause and Effect

Authors use cause and effect to explain how events and ideas relate to one another. A factor that makes one or more things happen is a cause. A result of one or more causes is an effect.

Understand Author's Purpose

Authors typically write for one or more of the following purposes: to persuade, to inform, to explain, to entertain, or to describe.

Find the Main Idea

The main idea is the most important idea in a paragraph or passage. Sometimes the main idea of a passage is stated in the first sentence. Sometimes it is stated in another place in the passage. Often, though, the main idea is implied. It is not actually stated but rather communicated indirectly through supporting details.

Unit 1 Assessment

Read each passage. Then circle the letter of the answer to each question.

Acupuncture began in China more than 4,500 years ago. Acupuncture is the practice of inserting needles into certain areas of the body to relieve pain or cure illness. The method is based on the idea that illness is caused by an imbalance of the body's forces. It is believed that the insertion of the needles causes the body to redirect those forces. Today, Chinese acupuncturists employ ancient charts that show where to insert the needles. Even modern practitioners are not exactly sure how the technique works. They do, however, recognize that inserting a needle in one place causes a specific reaction in another place.

1. What is a good paraphrase for the last two sentences in the passage?

   A   Inserting a needle in one place in the body causes a reaction somewhere else, even though no one knows exactly why.

   B   Modern practitioners don't understand how to insert a needle into the body.

   C   Acupuncture works because inserting a needle into one place in the body causes a specific reaction in another part.

   D   Modern practitioners are skeptical of acupuncture because they don't believe that inserting a needle in one place causes a specific reaction in another.

I believe that the wind turbine project would be beneficial for our area. Over time, our energy needs have grown, and wind turbines are an excellent way to produce energy. Wind is clean, free, and renewable. Also, unlike solar power, wind is available both day and night. Even light winds will generate some electricity. The strong winds coming from the mountain ranges in this area are, therefore, especially suitable for wind turbines. Voting yes on the wind turbine bill will benefit the town and the planet.

2. According to the writer, what is one benefit of wind turbines over solar energy collectors?

   F   Wind is clean, free, and renewable, unlike solar energy.

   G   Solar power panels are big and unsightly, but wind turbines have an inherent beauty.

   H   Strong winds from the mountain range will provide more power than solar power can.

   J   Wind turbines can run both day and night, while solar power can only be collected during daylight.

3. What is the writer's main purpose in writing this passage?

   A   to persuade readers that they use too much energy

   B   to persuade readers to vote in favor of a wind turbine bill

   C   to describe how wind turbines work

   D   to describe a source of clean energy

Many people don't realize that concrete and cement are not the same material. Cement is a chemical powder that forms a paste when mixed with water, and it is commonly used to make concrete. Concrete is a mixture of cement, water, sand, gravel, and crushed stone. The cement and water in the mixture hold the other materials together. Concrete can be molded into any shape and hardens very quickly. This extremely strong material is mainly used for buildings, roadways, dams, and other structures.

4. What is the best summary of this passage?

F Cement is a chemical powder that is mixed with other materials to form concrete. Concrete is a strong material that is used to build large buildings and other structures.

G Cement is a powder that is mixed with water, sand, gravel, and crushed stone to make concrete. Most large structures in a city are made of concrete.

H Concrete is made of cement. It is used in molds and is very strong.

J Builders use concrete to make many structures because it can be molded into many shapes. Concrete hardens quickly into an extremely strong material.

5. What conclusion can you draw about why many people think concrete and cement are the same material?

A Because the words start with the same letter, many people use them interchangeably.

B Many people don't know the difference between cement and gravel.

C Because cement is rarely used in mixtures other than concrete, many people think they are the same substance.

D Many people have been taught to believe that concrete and cement are the same.

To protect against fire or shock, every electrical system in your home includes one of two types of safety devices: a fuse or a circuit breaker. They operate differently but serve the same purpose—to stop the flow of electric current. Too much current can flow through a circuit when one circuit is used for too many appliances or electrical devices. A burned-out, or blown, fuse must be replaced with a new fuse before the current can flow through a circuit again. Circuit breakers trip, or break the circuit, by automatically snapping open to stop the flow of electrical current. The circuit breaker is then reset by hand, usually by flipping a lever.

6. What might cause a fuse to blow or a circuit breaker to trip?

F plugging 20 appliances into a single outlet

G leaving an appliance plugged in too long

H having too many circuits in your home

J failing to pay your electric bill

7. You can conclude from this passage that before replacing a fuse or resetting a circuit you should

A stop the flow of electrical current.

B protect yourself against fire or shock.

C determine the cause of the trouble and correct it.

D understand that circuit breakers and fuses are more trouble than they are worth.

It is critical to the survival of our video store that you properly scan in returned DVDs. For one thing, if a DVD is not scanned in, our inventory will not be accurate. A customer calling about a movie may be told that we do not have it, even if it is sitting on the shelf. Even worse, customers who correctly return a disc on time may be unfairly accused of not returning a disc and charged for it. As a result, our reputation will be hurt, and customers will stop using our store.

8. What is the writer's purpose for writing this passage?

F to explain why customers get angry if DVDs are not scanned in properly

G to persuade employees to scan in returned DVDs properly

H to describe the correct procedure for scanning in DVDs

J to describe the correct way to interact with customers returning DVDs

9. What is the main idea of this passage?

A The video store will close if returned DVDs are not scanned in correctly.

B It is important to scan returned DVDs in correctly.

C Customers will not be happy if mistakes are made concerning returned DVDs.

D The video store wants its reputation to remain intact.

Summer is the time for picnics in the park, vacations, and sunny days at the beach. Unfortunately, it is also the season of heat-related illnesses. Minor ailments include headache and nausea, while a more serious illness caused by too much heat is heatstroke. Evidence shows that heatstroke is caused by the failure of the body to cool itself off by sweating. This condition can happen when a person works or exercises for a prolonged period in hot temperatures, causing the body's heat-regulating mechanisms to become too fatigued to produce sweat. Without the evaporation of sweat to cool it, the body builds up too much heat. People with heat exhaustion, which is a mild version of heatstroke, can find relief by resting in a cool place and drinking liquids. Heatstroke, however, can cause loss of consciousness and, in extreme cases, death.

10. Heat exhaustion is a mild version of

F the flu.

G evaporation.

H sweating.

J heatstroke.

11. What is one effect of heatstroke?

A working too long in the sun

B drinking liquids

C loss of consciousness

D resting in a cool place

Read the bulletin board notice. Then circle the letter of the answer to each question.

Annual Cancer Walk!

The annual Walk for the Win is coming up on October 25. As you know, this walk raises money for cancer research, and Smith and Hines is proud to be a corporate sponsor of this worthwhile cause.

We hope Smith and Hines employees will participate in the walk this year. We have created teams for each department, and we urge you and your colleagues to sign up under your department. Also, don't forget that family and friends are welcome to sign up on our teams. All participants are encouraged to ask additional family and friends to sponsor their walk. In the spirit of friendly competition, Smith and Hines will award a prize to the team that raises the most money.

To register, visit the Walk for the Win website. Search for Smith and Hines, find your department, and join that team. Each department should designate a team captain to track the department's fundraising. Team captains should pick up the walk T-shirts for their department by October 23.

12. What is a good paraphrase of the first paragraph?

F Smith and Hines is a corporate sponsor of Walk for the Win. The walk raises money for cancer research and will be held October 25.

G The Walk for the Win is held annually. This year it will be on October 25.

H Smith and Hines is proud to sponsor Walk for the Win. It is a walk to raise money for cancer research.

J Smith and Hines will sponsor Walk for the Win on October 25.

13. How do employees and their family and friends register for the walk?

A They tell their department captain.

B They have their friends and family sponsor them.

C They sign up on the Smith and Hines website.

D They find their department on the Walk for the Win website.

14. What do you think the author's purpose was for writing this notice?

F to persuade employees to donate money to cancer research

G to persuade employees to sign up for the walk

H to explain how to sign up on the walk website

J to explain the need for money to fund cancer research

15. What is the main idea of the second paragraph?

A There is a competition to see which department can raise the most money.

B Everyone is required to sign up and find sponsors.

C A prize will be awarded for fundraising.

D Everyone is encouraged to participate and bring family and friends to the walk.

Read the procedural document. Then circle the letter of the answer to each question.

Holiday Extended Hours

Beginning December 12, the Shoppingtown Mall will go into extended holiday hours. All stores in the mall are required to be open during these hours to accommodate increased shopping traffic. In compliance with the mall's requirement, we will be extending our operating hours. Managers should begin interviewing additional seasonal employees, and all managers and sales associates should expect to work additional shifts. We appreciate your flexibility during this hectic time. Please review the calendar below to see the extended hours and begin to plan accordingly. Call the management office with any questions.

Sunday	Monday	Tuesday	Wednesday	Thursday	Friday	Saturday
December 12	December 13	December 14	December 15	December 16	December 17	December 18
10 A.M.–7 P.M.	9 A.M.–10 P.M.	9 A.M.–10 P.M.	9 A.M.–10 P.M.	9 A.M.–10 P.M.	9 A.M.–10 P.M.	9 A.M.–10 P.M.
December 19	December 20	December 21	December 22	December 23	December 24	December 25
9 A.M.–8 P.M.	8 A.M.–11 P.M.	8 A.M.–11 P.M.	8 A.M.–11 P.M.	8 A.M.–11 P.M.	8 A.M.–6 P.M.	CLOSED

16. What conclusion can you draw about why the mall stays open late despite the hassle for both stores and employees?

   F   The mall management is indifferent to employees' schedules.

   G   The mall management hopes the increased business will make up for the extra expense and difficulty of keeping the mall open.

   H   The mall management does not really expect all stores to stay open late. They just want to provide an option for stores that wish to remain open.

   J   The mall management hopes most shoppers will do their shopping early in the morning or late at night.

17. What is one effect of the extended holiday hours?

   A   All stores will stay open until 11 P.M. every night.

   B   Employees will need to work extra shifts.

   C   Management appreciates employees' flexibility.

   D   Extended hours will begin on December 12.

18. For how many days are the extended hours in effect?

   F   4

   G   6

   H   13

   J   14

19. Managers should begin interviewing

   A   full-time employees.

   B   part-time managers.

   C   seasonal employees.

   D   security guards.

20. What should employees do if they have questions about the extended hours?

   F   write an e-mail to the management office

   G   ask managers they know from other stores or restaurants

   H   call the management office

   J   close at the normal closing time

Circle the letter of the answer to each question.

21. Which word means "a person who sails"?

  A sailist

  B sailer

  C sailor

  D saileor

22. Which is the correct meaning of *triple-decker*?

  F a type of gymnastic move

  G an instrument in an orchestra

  H a special deck of cards

  J an item having three levels

23. Which form of *repeat* is spelled correctly?

  A repeatted

  B repeated

  C reppeating

  D repeatting

24. Which is the correct meaning of *energetic*?

  F like energy

  G without energy

  H tends to have energy

  J to move with energy

25. Which phrase means "the rosebushes belonging to the neighbors"?

  A the neighbors's rosebushes

  B the neighbors rosebushes

  C the neighbor's rosebushes

  D the neighbors' rosebushes

26. Which word fits into both sentences?

The brochure provided some _____ information about the military.

Frank was promoted to the rank of _____ after many years in the army.

  F general

  G complete

  H captain

  J specific

27. Which is the correct contraction for the words *would have*?

  A wouldve'

  B wouldv'e

  C would've

  D would'have

28. Which is the correct meaning of *distrust*?

  F trust strongly

  G trust less

  H not trust

  J trust more

29. Which is the correct plural form of *discovery*?

  A discoveries

  B discoveryies

  C discoverys

  D discovery's

30. Which word best completes the analogy?

Trumpet : musician as *hammer* : _____

  F singer

  G carpenter

  H teacher

  J professor

31. Which two words are homophones?

  A bread, brood

  B cling, clank

  C pause, paws

  D shirt, short

32. Which word is a synonym for the word *excited*?

  F bored

  G thrilled

  H angry

  J thirsty

Unit 2

In this unit you will learn how to

You will practice the following workplace skills

You will also learn new words and their meanings and put your reading skills to work in written activities. You will get additional reading practice in *Reading Basics Advanced Reader.*

Lesson 2.1

Identify Sequence

When you read, it is important to determine the order in which things happen. This time order, or sequence, will help you understand how events, concepts, and themes relate to one another. Sequence is present both in fiction and nonfiction. Some things you read may be narrative; that is, they tell a story. However, even passages that do not tell a story often have sequence.

Information in a passage may be presented in the order in which events happened, or it may be presented in a different order. Some words signal time order, such as *first, before, next, after, last,* and *then.* These clue words can help you identify sequence. Look for the clue words *first, then, when,* and *finally* as you read the example:

> First, an adult female butterfly lays her eggs on a suitable plant. The larva hatches from the egg and then eats the eggshell before moving on to other kinds of nearby food. Then it spends a few weeks eating and growing, shedding its exoskeleton each time it becomes too tight. When the larva is finished growing, it drops a silky liquid that hardens into a pad. The creature, now a pupa, grabs on to the pad with a special claw, hanging downward from the pad by a thread. A hard shell forms around it, and now it is a chrysalis. Finally, after many changes occur in the chrysalis, the adult butterfly emerges and spreads its wings.

Sometimes a writer does not use signal words to indicate sequence. Instead, he or she simply presents events and allows the reader to interpret the writing and determine the order of events on his or her own.

Read the passage. Underline the event that happened first. Circle the event that happened last.

> The original London Bridge was built in 1209 and lasted 622 years. It saw the bubonic plague come and go, survived the Great Fire of London, and suffered through stages of neglect and renovation. When repairing the bridge became impossible, a new bridge was built in 1831. That bridge did not last as long as the first one, and it now stands in Lake Havasu City, Arizona. Starting in 1968 the bridge was taken apart in London, shipped, and rebuilt in its new location.

The events in this passage are written in the order they occurred, and there are dates to help you identify the sequence as well. You should have underlined *The original London Bridge was built in 1209* because it happened first. You should have circled *rebuilt in its new location* because it is the last event described in this passage.

Read the passage. The events from the following passage are listed in incorrect order below it. Use the graphic organizer to put the events in the order they happened.

On Thursday, December 1, 1955, a seamstress and civil rights activist named Rosa Parks was asked to give up her seat on a bus to a white man. She was told to move to the back of a Montgomery, Alabama, bus. She quietly refused. Her subsequent arrest began a 381-day bus boycott that helped launch the civil rights movement in the United States. At the same time, it also helped launch the career of the civil rights leader Martin Luther King, Jr. Both Rosa Parks's arrest and the bus boycott became vehicles for drawing attention to the rights of African Americans. After Rosa Parks was convicted, her case was appealed to the U.S. Supreme Court. The court ruled that discrimination on buses violated federal law.

Rosa Parks was arrested.

Rosa Parks's case was appealed to the Supreme Court.

A 381-day bus boycott began.

Rosa Parks was asked to give up her seat on a bus to a white man.

The Supreme Court ruled that discrimination on buses violated federal law.

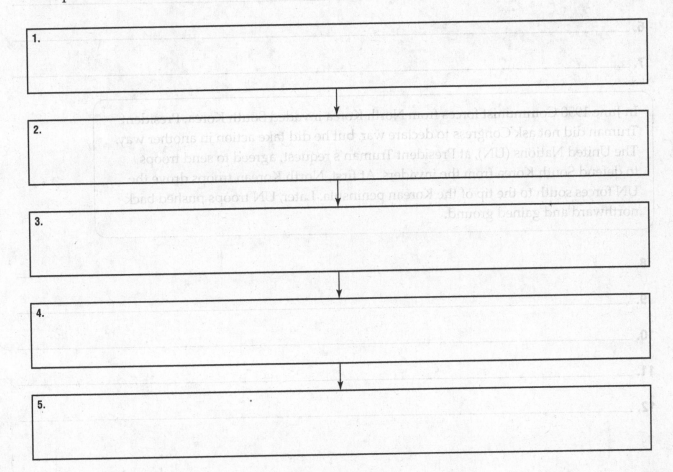

1.

2.

3.

4.

5.

Read each passage. Then write the events from the passage in order.

When a lake first forms, its water is clear and contains few organisms, but almost immediately the lake begins filling with microscopic organisms, seeds, and bits of decayed plants and animals. Soon animals such as insects, fish, and birds will move into the water. Inevitably, debris collects at the bottom of the lake. The buildup on a lake bottom is slow but steady—perhaps no more than a foot in 100 years—but eventually, plants take root in the sediments and speed the formation of new soil. Over time the lake becomes a wetland, such as a marsh or a swamp. As sediment continues to build up, the lake will fill in completely.

1. _____

2. _____

3. _____

4. _____

5. _____

6. _____

7. _____

In June 1950 Communist forces from North Korea invaded South Korea. President Truman did not ask Congress to declare war, but he did take action in another way. The United Nations (UN), at President Truman's request, agreed to send troops to defend South Korea from the invaders. At first, North Korean troops drove the UN forces south to the tip of the Korean peninsula. Later, UN troops pushed back northward and gained ground.

8. _____

9. _____

10. _____

11. _____

12. _____

Read the passage. Then circle the letter of the answer to each question.

The practice of dentistry has experienced many changes throughout the centuries. The ancient Phoenicians attempted to replace missing human teeth with animal teeth. The earliest gold dental bridges come from the Etruscans and date from before 600 B.C. In the Middle Ages, barbers served as both surgeons and dentists. In England, with a charter from Henry VIII, a guild for barbers and surgeons was established. The first English book on dentistry, *The Operator for the Teeth*, was published in 1685, but it wasn't until 1840 that the first professional dental school in the world was founded in Baltimore, Maryland. Dentists introduced anesthesia for extractions and other operations in 1844, and since then there have been many advances in dental techniques.

1. Who were the earliest known people to try to replace human teeth?

   A   the Etruscans

   B   the ancient Phoenicians

   C   dentists in Maryland

   D   members of the English guild of barbers and surgeons

2. Which of these events happened first?

   F   *The Operator for the Teeth* was published.

   G   The guild for barbers and surgeons was created.

   H   The Etruscans created gold dental bridges.

   J   Anesthesia was introduced for extractions.

3. When was the first professional dental school founded?

   A   600 B.C.

   B   1685

   C   1840

   D   1844

4. Who did the work of dentists in the Middle Ages?

   F   teachers

   G   barbers

   H   priests

   J   blacksmiths

5. When was the guild for barbers and surgeons established?

   A   before the earliest gold dental bridges

   B   after the first professional dental school was founded

   C   before dentists introduced anesthesia for extractions and other operations

   D   during the same time people were replacing human teeth with animal teeth

6. What happened after dentists introduced anesthesia?

   F   Henry VIII gave a charter for a guild for barbers and surgeons.

   G   The first English book on dentistry was published.

   H   The first dental school was established.

   J   Many advances in dental technique occured.

7. When were the first gold dental bridges used?

   A   before 600 B.C.

   B   1840

   C   1844

   D   after the first dental school opened

Workplace Skill:
Identify Sequence in Instructions

Workplace documents such as procedures, instructions, and processes are usually arranged in time sequence. Following the order correctly is an important part of successfully completing workplace tasks and responsibilities. Understanding the purpose of a sequence or procedure can make it easier to remember the steps.

Read the handout from the ORION Enterprises IT Department. Then circle the letter of the answer to each question below the box.

Guidelines for Backing Up Your Files from
ORION Enterprises IT Department

Backing up a file is making an extra copy of the file and storing it in a different location from the original. Backing up protects you from losing data due to viruses, computer malfunction, or human error. To protect your files from being lost, ee strongly suggest that you back up any files that relate to your work or other projects. If your computer malfunctions, your files won't be lost permanently. You can back up your files to another drive, your network, or a DVD.

Backing up files on Windows XP

- To begin backing up your files, click the *Start* menu button and select *All Programs/ Accessories/System Tools/Backup*.

- When you see the *Backup or Restore Wizard* window, click *Next* and then choose *Back up files and settings*.

- Click the *Next* button, and you should be on the *What to Back Up* screen.

- Select *Let me choose what to back up* and then, in the *Items to Back Up* window, choose the files or folders you want to back up and click *Next*.

- Specify the location where you want to store the backed-up files and then click *Finish*.

- When the files are backed up, click *Close* to end the process.

---

1. What should you do right before you click *Finish*?

  A Click *Close* to end the process.

  B Choose the files or folders you want to back up.

  C Specify the location to store the backed-up files.

  D Select *Let me choose what to back up*.

2. Which of the following can you infer about the purpose of this handout?

  F The IT Department wants to explain how files are lost.

  G The company wants to blame employees for ruining files.

  H The company wants the IT Department to back up files.

  J The company wants to address its concerns about protecting information.

Write for Work

Imagine that you are having trouble backing up your files at work and need help from someone in the IT Department. In a notebook, write a brief e-mail or set of numbered summarizing the steps you took to back up your files. You may refer to page 82. Use sequence and transition words such as *first, next, then*, and *finally* to make clear the order of the steps you followed.

 ## Reading Extension

Turn to "Tiger Trainers: Schooling the Big Cat" on page 41 of *Reading Basics Advanced Reader*. After you have read and/or listened to the article, answer the questions below.

Circle the letter of the answer to each question.

1. What is the first step to becoming a tiger trainer?

    A   earn a degree in animal training

    B   work as a backup trainer

    C   clean the tiger cages

    D   go into the tiger cages and let the animals get used to you

2. What do you need to do before you can understand tigers?

    F   give rewards and affection to them

    G   use positive and negative rewards

    H   spend thousands of hours with them

    J   give specific commands followed by rewards

3. When did a tiger maul an experienced trainer at the San Francisco Zoo in 2006?

    A   before the trainer fed the tiger

    B   while the trainer was feeding the tiger

    C   after the trainer fed the tiger

    D   while the trainer was cleaning the tiger's cage

Write the answer to each question.

4. What does Bhagavan Antle say might happen to tigers as they mature?

_____

_____

5. What happened to Roy Horn right after he fell on stage?

_____

_____

Explore Words

PREFIXES en-, em-

A prefix is a word part that can be added to the beginning of many words. Adding prefixes to base words changes their meanings. The prefixes *en-* and *em-* mean "to put in" or "to make or cause." For example, the word *entomb* means "to put in a tomb," and the word *enrich* means "to make rich."

Match each word on the left with its meaning on the right. Write the letter of the meaning next to the word.

_____ **1.** enrage   **a.** to put into power

_____ **2.** enable   **b.** to make dear

_____ **3.** encode   **c.** to cause rage

_____ **4.** ensure   **d.** to make tangled

_____ **5.** empower   **e.** to put into battle

_____ **6.** endear   **f.** to put into code

_____ **7.** entangle   **g.** to make able

_____ **8.** embattle   **h.** to make sure

SUFFIXES -ion, -tion

A suffix is a word part that can be added to the end of many words. Adding suffixes changes the meaning of the words to which they are added. The suffixes *-ion* and *-tion* mean "the result of" or "the act of." The word *education* means "the act of educating" or "the result of educating."

Write a word with the suffix *-ion* or *-tion* that has the meaning given.

1. the result of decorating _____

2. the act of discussing _____

3. the result of attracting _____

4. the result of complicating _____

5. the result of adopting _____

6. the act of inspecting _____

Some words have more than one meaning. For example, a *seal* is a marine animal. Used another way, *seal* also means "to close tightly." You can use context clues—other words in the same or nearby sentences—to figure out which meaning is intended.

Use context clues in each sentence that help you know the intended meaning of the underlined word. Circle the letter of the intended meaning.

1. Traffic on the interstate is being <u>diverted</u> because of an accident.

   a. changed from the usual route or path

   b. amused or entertained

2. Some people who are color-blind can't <u>discriminate</u> red from green.

   a. make a clear distinction

   b. act on the basis of prejudice

3. It looks like my license will <u>expire</u> next month.

   a. cease to live

   b. no longer be valid

4. My father plans on <u>retiring</u> when he is 70 years old.

   a. stopping work

   b. shy and modest

5. Please don't automatically <u>discount</u> what I am telling you.

   a. reduce the price of

   b. disregard or ignore

6. Have you <u>exhausted</u> every idea that the committee came up with?

   a. completely used up

   b. extremely tired

Knowing these high-frequency words will help you in many school subjects.

sequence	the order in which things happen
interpret	to explain the meaning of something
inevitable	certain to happen
subsequent	following
violate	to fail to comply with a rule

Complete the sentences below using one of the words above.

1. The poem was abstract and difficult to _____.

2. The dance teacher taught her class a difficult _____ of steps.

3. Sayid knew that if he adopted a dog, he would _____ his rent agreement.

4. Every member of her family is nearsighted, so it was _____ that Issa would need glasses.

5. Carmen's promotion and _____ raise were well deserved.

Lesson 2.2

Understand Consumer Materials

A consumer is someone who buys or uses goods and services, including food, clothing, and car repairs, for his or her own use. All people are consumers, whether they consume a lot or a little. People consume goods and services they need as well as those they want.

Printed materials are often associated with what you buy. These are called consumer materials. There are many different kinds of consumer materials, including advertisements, coupons, product labels, instructions, and owner's manuals. It is important to read consumer materials carefully and thoroughly. They may contain crucial information that you need to use or maintain your product or service, or they may contain information you need for the safety of the product or yourself.

The most common way to learn about a product or service is through advertisements. Below are some key points to keep in mind when you read advertisements.

- Read the description carefully.
- Investigate the seller's claims.
- Read restrictions and limitations carefully.
- Compare the offer with other products and other businesses' offers.

Study the ads. Write in a notebook which features are different between the two brands.

Clear Picture 32-in LCD HDTV
1080p Resolution
Clear Voice technology
1-year parts warranty
1-year labor warranty
$379

SurroundoPlex 32-in LCD HDTV
720p Resolution
Surround sound
1-year parts warranty
1-year labor warranty
$327

The three differences are price, resolution, and an additional feature. The Clear Picture brand television has Clear Voice technology but does not have surround sound. The SurroundoPlex brand television does not have Clear Voice technology, but it does have surround sound. Clear Picture's resolution is higher than SurroundoPlex's, but the price of the television is higher. As a consumer, you must decide which features you prefer and whether the better resolution is worth paying the higher price.

As a consumer, you may need to return items you purchased online, from a catalog, or over the phone. Most companies allow mail-in returns, but you will probably have to fill out a paper or electronic form with your return.

Suppose you bought a swimsuit from an online store, but now you want to return it. The swimsuit is too small, and you also don't like the design as much as you did when you saw it on the website.

Read the form. Then answer the questions.

```
┌──────────────────────────────────────────────────────────────────────────┐
│  Sea Glass Swimwear                    CONSUMER SERVICE CARD               │
│                                                                            │
│  Name _____        Date _____               │
│                                                                            │
│  Address _____       Order # _____               │
│                                                                            │
│  Item # ____ Color ____ Size ____ Qty. ____   Phone _____        │
│                                                                            │
│  Do you want to:    [  ] return?       [  ] credit account   [  ] refund money │
│                     [  ] exchange?                                         │
│                                                                            │
│  What are the problems with the merchandise?                               │
│  [  ] too big              [  ] doesn't look like picture                  │
│  [  ] too small            [  ] other (Please explain below.)              │
│  [  ] wrong color          _____            │
│  [  ] didn't like fabric   _____            │
└──────────────────────────────────────────────────────────────────────────┘
```

1. What does "Qty." stand for?

_____

2. How would you comment about the swimsuit's size?

_____

3. Where would you put your comment about the swimsuit's design?

_____

4. How do you decide whether to return or exchange the item?

_____

5. What are some of the advantages of ordering merchandise online?

_____

6. What are some of the disadvantages of ordering merchandise online?

_____

Some ratings systems use a grid to give information and compare products. It is a good idea to read the rankings as well as any comments left by reviewers.

Read the ratings chart. Then answer the questions.

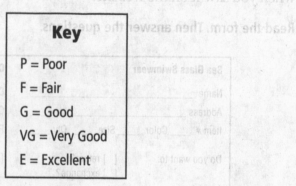

Ratings for Macaroni and Cheese

Product	Flavor and Texture	Comments
	P F G VG E	
Timesaver		Strong cheese flavor
Momma's		Thick sauce, low salt
Eddie's		Thin sauce, little cheese flavor
Healthy Heart		Low fat content, tiny shell pasta, good cheese flavor

Key

P = Poor
F = Fair
G = Good
VG = Very Good
E = Excellent

1. What words do the letters in the chart under "Flavor and Texture" represent?

_____

2. Aside from the flavor and texture rating, what other item on the chart can help you decide which brand to buy?

_____

3. If you like a thick sauce, which brand might you choose?

_____

4. If you are on a low-fat diet, which brand might you choose?

_____

5. If you only like large macaroni, which brand would NOT be a good choice for you?

_____

6. Which brand has the highest overall rating?

_____

7. Which brand has the lowest overall rating?

_____

Read the prescription label. Then circle the letter of the answer to each question.

1. What does RX# stand for?

   A referral exam number

   B prescription number

   C expiration date

   D doctor's phone number

2. When should you stop taking the penicillin?

   F after two days

   G when you feel better

   H when you have taken all the pills

   J never

3. How many refills are you allowed?

   A 0

   B 2

   C 10

   D 20

4. How should you take the medicine?

   F Take two pills in the morning and two at night.

   G Take one pill in the morning and one in the evening.

   H Take one pill each day.

   J Take two pills once per week.

5. How many pills are supplied?

   A 2

   B 20

   C 23

   D 250

6. Letter J points to

   F the address of the pharmacy.

   G the expiration date of the medicine.

   H the instructions for how to take the medicine.

   J the number of pills in the bottle.

7. Letter D points to

   A the patient's name.

   B the name of the doctor who prescribed the medicine.

   C the name of the medicine.

   D the name of the pharmacists.

8. Which letter indicates the date on which the prescription was written?

   F A

   G C

   H G

   J J

Workplace Skill: Understand Consumer Materials by Interpreting a Warranty

Consumer materials are documents that are written for the consumers, or purchasers, of goods or services. They can consist of the warranties, instructions, and safety information that are included when you purchase a product or service. At work, you need to understand the conditions and time limits on a warranty before giving customers repairs, replacements, or refunds on goods and services.

Read the warranty. Then circle the letter of the answer to each question below the box.

Edna's Auto Body Shop
WARRANTY

This certificate guarantees that the repairs for which you have contracted with Edna's Auto Body Shop have been finished. We stand behind our work at Edna's Auto Body Shop for as long as the repaired vehicle stays under its present ownership. This warranty applies only to defects that result from normal driving conditions. Damages from accidents, misuse, poor driving, or weather conditions are not covered. Any metalwork used to repair accident damage will be repaired and repainted if it flakes or deteriorates. If we apply paint over your original factory finish, our paint is guaranteed against blistering, hazing, and fading. We will repaint sections of the vehicle as needed.

Name _____

Warranty No. _____   Repair Order No. _____

Vehicle _____   Repair Date _____

Authorization Signature _____

---

1. Which of the following is covered under the warranty?

   A paint that blisters after the customer sells his or her vehicle

   B a dent caused by a branch falling on the customer's vehicle

   C metalwork that is damaged in an accident after the repair

   D paint that fades after it is applied over the factory finish

2. What is the most likely reason that Edna's has a warranty?

   F so that customers understand what work they can ask Edna's to correct

   G so that customers know that Edna's is not responsible for their work

   H so that customers will come to Edna's to have their car repainted each year

   J so that customers will drive their vehicles more cautiously after they have them repaired

Write for Work

Imagine that you are an employee of Edna's Auto Body. A customer had her car repainted at Edna's Auto Body after an accident. Now, six months later, her large key chain has scratched the door, and the customer thinks that Edna's Auto Body should repaint her car for free. In a notebook, write a letter or e-mail to the customer granting or denying her request. Use language and examples from the warranty on page 90 to support your response.

 Reading Extension

Turn to "Bull Riders: Ride or Run!" on page 49 of *Reading Basics Advanced Reader*. After you have read and/or listened to the article, answer the questions below.

Circle the letter of the answer to each question.

1. According to the article, what is one rule for men riding bulls?

   A They can only ride bulls that are 10 times as heavy as they are.

   B They can only use one hand.

   C The bulls have to be five years old.

   D They get extra points if their bull is prodded before the ride.

2. According to the article, what causes the bulls to buck?

   F They hate being cooped up in a stall.

   G They are trying to get the rider off their backs.

   H They are trying to kick a rope off their bellies.

   J They are angry that they have been prodded.

3. According to the article, how has the sport of bull riding been able to reach more consumers?

   A through fliers

   B through print ads

   C through television and digital media

   D through cheaper tickets

Write the answer to each question.

4. What is one injury faced by bull riders?

   _____

5. After reading this article, what is your opinion of bull riding?

   _____

Explore Words

Write for Work

LATIN ROOTS

Many English words have Latin roots. Knowing the meanings of roots can help you figure out the meanings of unfamiliar words. Read these common Latin roots, their meanings, and examples of English words using them.

port	"carry"	*portable* (able to be carried)
tain	"hold"	*contain* (hold together)

Write two words that have the Latin root *port* and two words that have the Latin root *tain*. Then find each word in a dictionary and write a brief definition in your own words.

1. _____

2. _____

3. _____

4. _____

WORD FAMILIES

A word family is a group of words that have the same base word. When you add prefixes, suffixes, and other word endings to a base word, the resulting words are members of the same word family. For example, the words *act, acted, acting, actor, action, react, reaction, active, activate,* and *deactivate* share the base word *act*. Therefore, these words form a word family.

Create three word family lists by writing each word in the box under one of the headings below.

disbelieve	approval	direction	redirected	unproved
disapproving	unbelievable	directory	believer	

1. direct

_____

_____

_____

2. believe

_____

_____

_____

3. approve

_____

_____

_____

Reading Basics · Advanced

ACCENTED AND UNACCENTED SYLLABLES

A syllable is a word part that has one vowel sound. In multisyllabic words, one of the syllables is accented, or stressed. Knowing syllable accent patterns can help you read and spell multisyllabic words.

- In two-syllable words, the accent is usually on the first syllable. The unaccented second syllable often has the schwa sound. The schwa sound is similar to the short *u* or short *i* sound. You can hear it in the second syllable of *these words:* hus/band, tal/ent, ti/tle. Every vowel can stand for the schwa sound. When you learn a new word, pay attention to the way the schwa sound is spelled.

- In two-syllable words that include a prefix, the accent is usually on the second syllable: de/stroy, re/veal, dis/like.

Divide each word into syllables and underline the accented syllable. The first item has been done for you.

1. misread ___*mis/read*___

2. enjoy _____

3. cottage _____

4. disrupt _____

5. slugger _____

6. trumpet _____

7. resell _____

8. fabric _____

ACADEMIC VOCABULARY

Knowing these high-frequency words will help you in many school subjects.

consume	to buy or use up
instructions	directions or orders
crucial	very important
maintain	to keep from failure or decline
common	seen often

Complete the sentences below using one of the words above.

1. If you keep business records electronically, you will _____ less paper.

2. Regular oil changes are important to _____ your car's engine.

3. The assembly _____ were easy to read, even without the pictures.

4. Li missed a _____ remark at the beginning, so she did not understand the rest of the lecture.

5. Jacobo thought he had found a rare stamp, but it turned out to be quite _____.

Lesson 2.3

Use Reference Sources

You may need to do research at different times. You may want to look up more information about someone famous or research a city you want to visit. You may need to do research for your job. All reference sources give information. The list below shows some of these sources and the type of information they provide.

encyclopedia	provides short articles with facts about almost all topics
thesaurus	lists synonyms, antonyms, and homonyms for words
Books in Print	lists all hardcover and paperback books (if they are still in print) by title, author, and subject
world atlas	provides maps and information about countries
world almanac	provides annually updated facts about countries, weather, people, events, and many other topics
Guinness World Records	provides records that were set by people and events around the world
Bartlett's Familiar Quotations	lists famous quotations and the people who said them

Many reference sources are available in both print form and online, although you may have to subscribe or pay a fee to use the online version. You may wish to use the Internet for research, either at home or at the library. Not all of the information you will find online is reliable. There are many websites that allow any user to add or modify content. You should not accept them as an authority without verifying the information in another source. Websites that are usually trustworthy include government websites and museum websites.

The library has reference books available for research set aside in a special section reserved for reference books. In general, you can use these books in the library, but you cannot check them out. Many of these books have a table of contents or index to help you find the information you need quickly. Many books have a glossary in the back to give definitions of specialized words used in the book. Don't be afraid to ask librarians to assist you. They are there to help you find resources and information.

Which reference book could you use to find the following information?

> a synonym for the word *lovely*   an antonym for the word *short*

You should have chosen a thesaurus. It gives synonyms and antonyms for words.

Libraries have catalogs that give information about the books in their collections. Many libraries use an online catalog. You can enter a title, author, or keywords, and the catalog will show all books related to your search. You will also see the book's call number, which tells you where the book is shelved. Some catalogs are on cards with three cards for each book—one by author, one by subject, and one by title. Whichever method you use to search, you will see the same basic information for a book.

Read each entry. Then answer the questions.

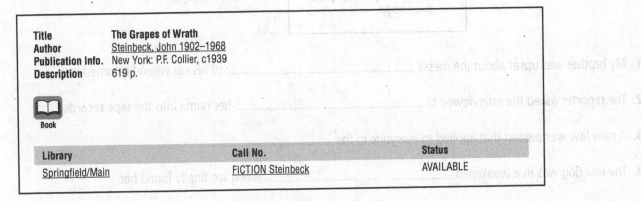

Title	The Grapes of Wrath
Author	Steinbeck, John 1902–1968
Publication Info.	New York: P.F. Collier, c1939
Description	619 p.

Book

Library	Call No.	Status
Springfield/Main	FICTION Steinbeck	AVAILABLE

1. What is the title of the book? _____

2. How many pages does the book have? _____

3. Is the book available at the library? Which one? _____

Title	The Seven Habits of Highly Effective People: Restoring the Character Ethic
Author	Covey, Stephen R.
Publication Info.	New York: Simon and Schuster, 1989
Description	340 p.: ill., 25 cm

Book

Library	Call No.	Status
Springfield/Main	158 COV	OUT

4. How many pages does the book have? _____

5. In what year was this book published? _____

6. Who is the publisher of the book? _____

Use the thesaurus entry below to choose a word that is a synonym for the word *state* to complete each sentence.

> **state** [*n1*] condition, situation, circumstances, position, shape
> **state** [*n2*] country, nation, land, kingdom, realm
> **state** [*v*] say, utter, declare, assert, announce
> **state** [*adj*] official, formal, public, governmental

1. My brother was upset about the messy _____ of his car when I returned it.

2. The reporter asked the interviewee to _____ her name into the tape recorder.

3. A new law was passed that applied to everyone in the _____.

4. The lost dog was in a weakened _____ when we finally found her.

5. On a(n) _____ visit to Japan, the president tried many local delicacies.

6. Karamo felt he had to _____ his opinion, even though no one asked.

7. In England the royal family acts as the head of the _____.

8. The White House held a _____ dinner for the visiting king.

Write four sentences using words that are found in the thesaurus entry for *state* above. Use each entry once.

9. _____

_____

10. _____

_____

11. _____

_____

12. _____

_____

Use what you know about reference materials to finish each of the following statements. Then circle the letter of each answer.

1. A library's online catalog entry would NOT include

   A   the book title.

   B   the author's name.

   C   the book's call number.

   D   at which bookstores the book is available.

2. You could find a synonym for a word in a(n)

   F   thesaurus.

   G   encyclopedia.

   H   card catalog.

   J   atlas.

3. If you are having trouble finding a particular book, you could look for publishing information in

   A   *Guinness World Records.*

   B   a biographical index.

   C   an encyclopedia.

   D   *Books in Print.*

4. You could find a detailed report about a famous person's life in

   F   an almanac.

   G   a thesaurus.

   H   an encyclopedia.

   J   *Guinness World Records.*

5. If you are looking up the main exports and total land area of Cuba, it would be helpful to look in all of these sources EXCEPT

   A   an encyclopedia.

   B   a thesaurus.

   C   a world almanac.

   D   an atlas.

6. To find information about the most Olympic medals won by an individual, you would look in

   F   an atlas.

   G   *Bartlett's Familiar Quotations.*

   H   *Guinness World Records.*

   J   *Books in Print.*

7. An almanac is published

   A   daily.

   B   monthly.

   C   yearly.

   D   every five years.

8. You would probably find the most information about Woodrow Wilson in

   F   an almanac.

   G   a biography of Wilson written by a history professor.

   H   a book about 20th-century U.S. presidents.

   J   an encyclopedia.

9. In which source would you look to find out who said, "Ask not what your country can do for you—ask what you can do for your country"?

   A   an almanac

   B   a card catalog

   C   a thesaurus

   D   *Bartlett's Familiar Quotations*

10. Which of these pieces of information would you find in an atlas?

   F   the date on which Abraham Lincoln was shot

   G   the scientific name of the Siberian tiger

   H   the major rivers in India

   J   a synonym for the word *cranky*

Workplace Skill:
Use Reference Sources to Locate Information

You might use a print or online encyclopedia at work to verify a fact or gather information about a topic. You might use a dictionary to help you find the meaning of a word or a thesaurus to help you choose just the right words to express your ideas.

Read the food-handling guidelines from Lickety Chick. Then circle the letter of the answer to each question below the box.

> At Lickety Chick, food safety is our number-one priority. Our consumers expect fresh, delicious chicken that is free from disease-causing bacteria, such as salmonella. The salmonella family of bacteria has about 2,000 different strains, but only 10 cause salmonella infections. Salmonellosis is preventable if routine food-safety practices are followed. Lickety Chick employees are expected to follow these food-handling guidelines:
>
> - Always sanitize hands with hot water and soap before handling food and after using the restroom. Rub soapy hands for at least 20 seconds before rinsing them.
>
> - All cutting boards, dishes, utensils, and countertops should be washed with hot, soapy water after preparing each food item and before moving on to the next. Sanitize your work space with a chlorine and water solution of one tablespoon of chlorine to one gallon of water.
>
> - Defrost food in the refrigerator—never at room temperature.
>
> - Never place cooked food on a plate or surface that held raw poultry.
>
> - Cook poultry parts to 170°F and whole chickens to 180°F. Use a clean thermometer to verify the internal temperature.

1. Which reference source would be the best way to verify the number of strains of salmonella?

   A a dictionary

   B a blog about food safety

   C an encyclopedia

   D a cooking website

2. If you do not understand the word *verify*, what reference source could you use to find the definition?

   F an encyclopedia

   G an atlas

   H a dictionary

   J an almanac

3. The word *sanitize* is used twice in this document. Which source would help you find a synonym?

   A a dictionary

   B a thesaurus

   C an encyclopedia

   D a medical website

4. If you want to learn more about what symptoms salmonella causes, what reference source could you use?

   F a dictionary

   G a thesaurus

   H a medical website

   J an almanac

Write for Work

Imagine that you are a kitchen manager at Lickety Chick. In a notebook, create a food-safety poster that reminds employees of the key points of the food-handling guidelines on page 98. Use a print or online encyclopedia to verify your facts and a print or online dictionary to check your spelling.

 **Reading Extension**

Turn to "Sherpas: Helpers in High Altitudes" on page 57 of *Reading Basics Advanced Reader*. After you have read and/or listened to the article, answer the questions below.

Circle the letter of the answer to each question.

1. In which reference source could you look up information about K2, Annapurna, and Mount Everest?

    A *Bartlett's Familiar Quotations*

    B a thesaurus

    C an encyclopedia

    D *Books in Print*

2. Which reference source would you look in to find out who has climbed Mount Everest the most times?

    F a world atlas

    G a world almanac

    H *Guinness World Records*

    J a dictionary

3. Which reference source could you use to find out how to treat hypothermia?

    A a dictionary

    B a thesaurus

    C a world almanac

    D a medical website

Write the answer to each question.

4. What is one reason Sherpas are well suited to be guides for climbers?

_____

5. What are some of the duties Sherpas perform on climbs?

_____

Explore Words

PREFIXES

A prefix is a word part that can be added to the beginning of many words. Adding a prefix to a base word or root changes its meaning. For example, the prefixes *co-*, *col-*, *com-*, *con-*, and *cor-* all mean "with" or "together." The form of the prefix used depends on the spelling of the base word or root that follows it.

Each word in the box includes one of these prefixes: *co-*, *col-*, *com-*, *con-*, and *cor-*. Choose a word to complete each sentence. Write the word and then circle the prefix.

complain	congratulate	collision
communicate	conference	correlation

1. Our meeting will be held at 9:00 A.M. in the _____ room.

2. The _____ caused almost $900 in damages to my car.

3. Studies show a _____ between eating breakfast and test scores.

4. Most kids _____ by texting each other these days.

5. Allow me to _____ you on your well-deserved promotion!

LATIN ROOTS

Many English words have roots from other languages, such as Latin. Latin roots have meanings. For example, the Latin root *ject* means "throw," and *tract* means "pull." Here are the meanings of some other common Latin roots.

dict	"say"	*spec* or *spect*	"look"
struct	"build"	*mit* or *miss*	"send"

Match each word on the left with its meaning on the right. Write the letter of the meaning next to the word.

_____ 1. intermittent   **a.** an extreme visual display

_____ 2. diction   **b.** occurring from time to time

_____ 3. speculation   **c.** a theory or guess

_____ 4. instructor   **d.** someone who teaches or instructs

_____ 5. spectacle   **e.** the style of speaking or singing

Some words have more than one meaning. For example, the word *volume* relates to the intensity of sound. It also means "a single book." You can use context clues—other words in the same or nearby sentences—to figure out which meaning is intended.

Use context clues in each sentence that help you know the intended meaning of the underlined word. Circle the letter of the intended meaning.

1. Saline <u>solution</u> is nothing but sterile salt water.

   a. a liquid mixture

   b. the answer to a problem

2. I love the <u>atmosphere</u> of a candlelit room.

   a. the gases that surround Earth

   b. the tone or mood of a place

3. Parents should take some <u>credit</u> for their children's success.

   a. pride for making a contribution

   b. buying with a promise to pay

4. Dr. Wu said that the patient was <u>stable</u> and resting comfortably.

   a. not likely to change for the worse

   b. a building where horses are kept

Knowing these high-frequency words will help you in many school subjects.

research	the organized study of materials and sources in order to find facts and draw conclusions
general	true for all or most instances
index	an alphabetical list of topics in a book or books and the pages on which they are found
available	able to be used or free to do something
assist	to help

Complete the sentences below using one of the words above.

1. There are many sizes and colors _____ in that sweater style.

2. Dashay asked a friend to _____ her in making her son's Halloween costume.

3. Marcos looked in the _____ to find out which page had the information he needed.

4. In _____ it is hot in the summer and cold in the winter.

5. Imelda enjoyed doing _____ but hated writing the report afterward.

Lesson 2.4

Use Supporting Evidence

Good writers do not simply state a generalization or an opinion. They must offer supporting evidence, which can be examples, facts, or statistics. Likewise, good readers should pay close attention to these kinds of supporting evidence. Evaluating the evidence helps readers decide whether the writer's opinion or generalization is valid. Some details may not support the main idea in the way the writer intended, and there may also be details that contradict the main idea. Additionally, there may be unrelated details that are irrelevant to the main idea. As a reader, you must eliminate the details that are not relevant to the main idea and then evaluate whether or not the details that remain are enough to support the writer's point. You must also consider the details that contradict the writer's point as you make your assessment. In the following example, the main idea is boldfaced. The sentences that follow it act as supporting evidence.

> **Birds will go to great extremes to protect their young.** They will attack intruders that normally they would try to avoid. Adult robins, both male and female, issue piercing cries of alarm and fly frantically about, sometimes "dive bombing" an invader. The usually peaceful swan may attack suddenly, striking out viciously with its beak and wings if its nest is threatened.

The first sentence of this passage is a general statement, and the writer supports it with examples that describe the behavior of two specific birds: robins and swans. The behaviors are out of the ordinary, and they support the idea that birds will go to extremes to protect their young.

Read the passage. Circle the main idea. Then underline the supporting evidence.

> There are strange stories about what several famous composers did to stimulate their creativity. Some say that Ludwig van Beethoven often moved because he felt that he could write better on certain sides of the street at different times. Wolfgang Amadeus Mozart supposedly composed his greatest works while playing billiards, and Richard Wagner would get into the spirit of his operas by wearing costumes while he composed. Many people say Mozart is their favorite composer.

You should have circled the first sentence. The sentences that follow the main idea provide examples that support the idea that there are strange stories about composers. The examples are supporting evidence. You should have underlined the second and third sentences. The fourth sentence is not relevant to the main idea.

Read each passage. Then underline the main idea. Write one detail, example, fact, or statistic from the passage that supports the main idea.

In the early days of movies, Mary Pickford was both a major Hollywood film star and a successful businesswoman. After years of working on stage, she began acting in films in 1909 when she was 16. Her blond curls and her ability to portray sweetness and innocence helped her to become known as America's sweetheart. However, Mary was also a skilled businesswoman. She formed Mary Pickford Studios and started producing her own movies. In 1919 she joined with Charlie Chaplin, Douglas Fairbanks, and D. W. Griffith to form United Artists. Today, United Artists is a major production company.

1. _____

_____

Social insurance programs give financial or other benefits to people who have made regular financial contributions to the program. The largest social insurance programs in the United States are Social Security and Medicare. Working people and their employers pay into these two programs, and upon retirement these retirees receive income and health benefits from the government.

2. _____

_____

Some hazardous wastes come from the products that we produce and use in our homes. A household hazardous waste is any product or chemical used in the home that contains toxic or corrosive ingredients. Leftover house paints are hazardous waste. Excess automotive oils and fluids, such as gasoline, brake fluid, motor oil, and windshield wiper fluid, are also considered harmful chemicals. Hazardous wastes include pesticides and poisons that are used to control insects and pests around homes and gardens. When we throw out old batteries, some light bulbs, computers, and television sets, we are throwing away hazardous waste.

3. _____

_____

Read each passage. Then write the answers to the questions.

Cities located near the equator don't always have hot temperatures. While some equatorial places, such as Singapore and Pontianak, Indonesia, have average low temperatures around 70°F, Quito, a city in Ecuador, is a very different case. This equatorial city has crisp year-round weather with average lows in the upper 40s. That's because Quito is located in the mountains, and its great elevation keeps it cool.

1. What city is used as an example to support the first sentence?

_____

2. Why does the author mention Singapore and Pontianak?

_____

Not too long ago, many illnesses raged across the United States. Smallpox, which was declared officially eliminated in 1980, swept across the Northeast in 1616, nearly wiping out whole Native American nations. Then from 1775 to 1782, during the American Revolution, smallpox claimed the lives of more than 100,000 people, including many soldiers, women, and children. Cholera struck the United States in 1832, killing many thousands of people, especially those people living in large cities. Polio, a crippling disease that at one time had no vaccine, claimed the lives of 123 victims in Vermont in 1894.

3. Name the diseases used as examples to support the first sentence of the passage.

_____

4. What statistics support the statement that smallpox was one of the illnesses that raged across the United States?

_____

5. What statistic support the statement that cholera was one of the illnesses that raged across the United States?

_____

_____

Read the passage. Then circle the letter of the answer to each question.

Television was not invented by a single person or company, but it was developed over many years through the work of numerous scientists and engineers. In 1817 a Swedish chemist found and named the element selenium, which conducts electricity strongly when it is exposed to light. Work with selenium led to the photoelectric cell, which converts light into electrical impulses. In 1884 a German engineer invented the mechanical television. In the 1920s scientists combined radio-broadcasting techniques with the mechanical television. An American and an Englishman separately developed picture transmission by combining photography, optics, and radio. More efficient systems, based on the work of these early scientists, were then built.

1. The first step in the development of television that is mentioned in the passage was

   A   the discovery of selenium.

   B   the invention of the photoelectric cell.

   C   experiments with electricity.

   D   the invention of radio.

2. The element selenium conducts electricity most when

   F   it is very cold.

   G   it is exposed to light.

   H   it is immersed in heat.

   J   it is left in darkness.

3. What event happened in 1884?

   A   A mechanical television was invented.

   B   The photoelectric cell was invented.

   C   The element selenium was discovered.

   D   Picture transmission was developed.

4. What is the main idea of this passage?

   F   More efficient televisions were built after the 1920s.

   G   A German engineer is the inventor of television.

   H   No one person invented television.

   J   Selenium was crucial to the invention of television.

5. What technique does the writer use to show supporting evidence for the main idea?

   A   using several unrelated examples

   B   using statistics

   C   describing the lives and works of several scientists

   D   tracing historical developments

Workplace Skill:
Use Supporting Evidence to Understand a Procedure

When you read memos, policies, and procedures, look for supporting evidence to help you understand the main ideas and what you should do with the information.

Look at the procedures for clocking in and out at a learning lab at State College. Then circle the letter of the answer to each question below the box.

Clocking In and Out

When you arrive at the learning lab to start your shift, go to the computer at the first workstation. Double click the "Time Clock" icon. Then click "Clock In" and select your name from the scroll-down menu. Click on your name and type in your password, and the exact time that you clocked in will appear. Confirm that the time is correct and then close the time clock toolbar by clicking on the "x" in the upper-right corner. When your shift is completed, repeat these steps except click "Clock Out." An employee is permitted to clock in a few minutes before or a few minutes after his or her normal starting and ending times. This is permitted as long as no work is performed during the time before or after this official start time. Managers should monitor this to limit it to only a few minutes before or after a shift.

If you forget to clock in or out, please do so as soon as you remember by typing in the correction, including the actual time you started or ended your shift, in the "note" section of the time sheet. In order to make sure you are paid accurately, we strongly recommend that you keep a personal record of the times when you clocked in and out and verify your time sheet before it is submitted to payroll. It can take as long as three pay cycles for corrections to be processed.

1. Which evidence best supports the importance of verifying your time sheet?

   A It can take as long as three pay cycles for corrections to be processed.

   B We strongly recommend that you keep a personal record of the times when you clocked in and out.

   C If you forget to clock in or out, please do so as soon as you remember.

   D Type the correction in the "note" section of the time sheet.

2. Why should employees note the correct times if they forget to clock in or out?

   F so that their supervisor will know they worked their shift

   G to make sure they aren't too late or too early for their shift

   H so that they are paid accurately for the time they worked

   J so that the clock on the computer system will not be wrong

Write for Work

Imagine you work in payroll and an employee sends you an e-mail telling you that his paycheck is incorrect. In a notebook, write a draft of an e-mail response to the employee explaining when he can expect the correction to be processed. Review the procedure for clocking in and out on page 106 and the importance of verifying the time sheet before it is turned in.

 ## Reading Extension

Turn to "Astronaut Mechanics: Hanging in Space" on page 65 of *Reading Basics Advanced Reader*. After you have read and/or listened to the article, answer the questions below.

Circle the letter of the answer to each question.

1. What is the main idea of this article?

   A Astronaut mechanics can cause damage and lose equipment.

   B Astronaut mechanics face many risks.

   C Astronaut mechanics always get their job done.

   D Space exploration is much safer than it used to be.

2. Which piece of evidence supports the main idea?

   F Feustel tried a socket wrench, but it did nothing to budge the bolt.

   G The new camera would allow the telescope to see even deeper into space.

   H Outer space has micrometeoroids that can puncture a spacesuit, causing an astronaut's entire oxygen supply to instantly escape.

   J The tragic explosion of the shuttle *Challenger* in 1986 killed all seven people on board.

Write the answer to each question.

3. Reread paragraph 3. Name one piece of evidence that supports the assertion that mechanics encounter danger from the extreme temperatures of space.

   _____

   _____

4. Reread paragraph 8. Name one piece of evidence that supports the assertion that seemingly small mishaps and slip-ups can turn into major problems in space.

   _____

   _____

Explore Words

SUFFIXES -ous, -ious

A suffix is a word part that can be added to the end of many words. Adding a suffix to a base word or root changes its meaning. For example, the suffixes *-ous* and *-ious* mean "characterized by" or "having the quality of." For example, the word *mountainous* means "characterized by mountains," and the word *infectious* means "characterized by infection."

Write the meaning of each word with the suffix *-ous* or *-ious*.

1. disastrous _____

2. anxious _____

3. cautious _____

4. mysterious _____

5. ambitious _____

6. glamorous _____

7. joyous _____

8. melodious _____

SPELLING: HOMOPHONES

Homophones are words that sound alike but are spelled differently and have different meanings. For example, *nose* and *knows* are homophones.

Circle the word that completes each sentence.

1. Have I ever (shone, shown) you this picture of my daughter?

2. Your (presents, presence) is requested in the conference room.

3. Please let me know (whether, weather) or not you can attend.

4. My library books are almost a week (overdue, overdo)!

5. Many cars have had problems with the gas (peddle, pedal).

6. Is Dr. Han taking new (patients, patience)?

7. Not many people use (stationary, stationery) to write letters these days.

8. I would love a hot-fudge (Sunday, sundae) right now!

9. The perfume has a strong but pleasant (scent, sent).

GREEK ROOTS

Many English words have Greek roots. Knowing the meaning of common Greek roots can help you figure out what unfamiliar words mean.

geo	"Earth"		*micro*	"small"
ology	"the study of"		*phon*	"sound"

Match each word on the left with its meaning on the right. Write the letter of the meaning next to the word. Use what you know about roots to help you.

1. _____ microscope
2. _____ microprint
3. _____ geology
4. _____ geologist
5. _____ phonics
6. _____ micromanage
7. _____ geode
8. _____ microphone

a. a crystal-filled rock

b. a system of sounds and letters

c. an instrument for seeing small objects

d. an instrument that makes sounds louder

e. tiny printed text

f. the study of Earth

g. to manage small details

h. a person who studies Earth

ACADEMIC VOCABULARY

Knowing these high-frequency words will help you in many school subjects.

evidence   facts or information that show whether something is true

support   to suggest that something is true or endorse it

example   something that illustrates a general rule

evaluate   to assess

irrelevant   not connected with something

Complete the sentences below using one of the words above.

1. The fact that Lebna is not wearing a suit is _____ to her competence at work.

2. The candidate should _____ the ballot initiative if she wants to win.

3. There is no _____ that the fire was the cause of the explosion.

4. It is difficult to _____ the talents of your own child.

5. Coffee is just one _____ of a breakfast drink.

Lesson 2.5

Recognize Character Traits

INTRODUCE

People in real life and characters in novels have character traits—ways of behaving, beliefs, physical characteristics, and patterns of speech. Fiction writers use narration, dialogue, and action to show character traits. Writers of nonfiction use some of these techniques to describe real people. There are several key techniques that authors employ to show character traits.

Narration: The author tells how the character looks, states the character's inner thoughts or feelings, or tells what other characters think about the main character.

Dialogue: The author tells what the characters say and how they say it. The author tells what other characters say about the main character.

Action: The author has the character do things that reveal his or her personality.

When you read you should analyze what the author is revealing through all of these various techniques so that you can recognize character traits and understand the character. Read the example below and note how the author has used character traits.

On a tour of France in 1961 Jacqueline Kennedy enchanted the French, who liked her elegance and her ability to speak their language. She received quite a bit of favorable newspaper coverage. On his last day in France, President John F. Kennedy said perhaps he should introduce himself. He said, "I am the man who accompanied Jacqueline Kennedy to Paris."

Through narration, the author tells what other people think about Jacqueline Kennedy and that she could speak French. Through dialogue, the author shows what another character, her husband, thinks about her. The reader can infer that Jacqueline Kennedy was educated, charismatic, and well liked by many people.

Read the passage. Note how the author reveals José's character.

At first the boy, not more than 18 and small, did not impress them. He said simply that he was José, and he wanted to work for the cause. This was all—not a wasted word of introduction. He stood without smiling, acting almost somber. Big, powerful Felipé stepped up to him and felt at once that something was wrong, something frightening. The boy's black eyes were like a snake's, and they burned like cold fire. José's eyes searched the room, from one face to another, but the others looked away.

In this passage, the author describes José's actions and appearance to communicate his cold, fearless, and rather frightening character.

Read each passage. Then write a word from the list that indicates the character trait revealed in each passage.

| obsession | ambition | anxiety |

Lahela never told anyone that she daydreamed about running while she was supposed to be thinking about schoolwork. She was impatient to go to high school because she knew there were high school track meets. Her tiny grammar school couldn't scrape the money together for real coaches, but the high school was much bigger, and it had real sports teams. Lahela had never been coached in track, and yet she could run faster than any other kid in her class. She could only imagine how fast she would be if she had some real coaching. No one would be able to catch her when she ran ahead of the pack, a tiny speck on the horizon.

1. _____

Kateri chose a special pen to write the inspirational quote at the bottom of the last page of the packet. She looked up where Dilip Ranjen's next concert was going to be and addressed her envelope to him in care of the night club. Before she sealed the envelope, she wrote her name and phone number on the bottom of the page. She hadn't included it in the last four packages, but she felt Dilip would finally be ready to call her, now that she had sent him her entire novel.

2. _____

Francesca checked the registration website again. It hadn't changed much in the last 10 minutes, but there was one less available seat in her first-choice class. She studied her handwritten list again, checking that she had written the course numbers down correctly. Her first choices were at the top, highlighted and starred, and she wanted to get into them really badly. She had researched the professors of all the classes she had been interested in, asking nearly every student she encountered. Her second-choice classes were okay, but they occurred at slightly less desirable times, and she wasn't as excited about them. It didn't even bear thinking about her third-choice classes. She hit refresh on the browser window and counted down the minutes until it was her turn to register.

3. _____

Read the following passage.

Emmett handed in his paper and exited the classroom, making no effort to be quiet or to keep from disturbing the other students still taking the test.

"Don't feel like you have to work as fast as Emmett," the teacher said after Emmett was outside. "Quicker doesn't always mean better."

The other students looked relieved and bent their heads back down over their essays. Some students looked confused about how anyone could finish an essay test as swiftly as Emmett always seemed to.

Emmett strolled around campus, enjoying the crisp autumn air and smiling to himself contentedly. He was certain he would get an A on his essay, even though he had finished it in less than half the time allotted. No one else he knew wrote as quickly as he did, and Emmett thought it was good to show the teacher that he could think faster than the other students. Emmett felt that quicker meant better almost all of the time.

In each bubble, write a word or phrase that describes Emmett.

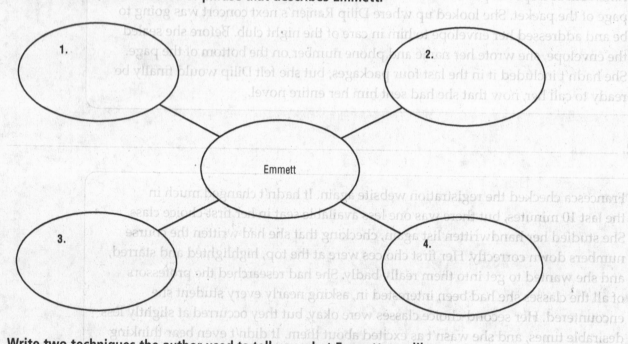

Write two techniques the author used to tell you what Emmett was like.

5. _____

6. _____

Read the passage. Then circle the letter of the answer to each question.

> Thomas Jefferson was the third U.S. president, chief author of the Declaration of Independence, and a strong supporter of the separation of church and state. He was also a noted architect, guiding the design of his estate at Monticello, a smaller home at Bedford, and the campus of the University of Virginia. Jefferson had great respect for farmers, saying "those who labor in the earth are the chosen people of God." As a farmer himself, he became an expert on agricultural techniques. As president, Jefferson oversaw the Louisiana Purchase, which doubled the size of the United States. He then authorized Lewis and Clark's expedition to explore the territory. He died on July 4, 1826, the 50th anniversary of Independence Day in the United States.

1. Jefferson's words and actions regarding farmers show that he
   A   said one thing and did another.
   B   thought farming was a valuable occupation.
   C   believed farming was for only uneducated people.
   D   did not spend much time thinking about farming.

2. Which of the following words does NOT accurately describe the character of Thomas Jefferson?
   F   bright
   G   curious
   H   narrow-minded
   J   talented

3. Jefferson's actions show that he
   A   considered politics the only worthwhile occupation.
   B   did not see the value in education.
   C   was highly motivated to discover new things.
   D   usually had other people do jobs for him.

4. Based on this passage, how would you describe Jefferson?
   F   demanding and temperamental
   G   scholarly and snobbish
   H   shy and isolated
   J   intelligent and well-rounded

5. How would you describe Jefferson's attitude toward expansion?
   A   He did not care about the West.
   B   He thought the United States was too large already.
   C   He wanted to expand the country.
   D   He thought the land he purchased was not worth living on.

Workplace Skill:
Evaluate Character Traits in a Performance Assessment Review

Companies use assessment forms to analyze workers' job performances. Eaton Publishing Company uses the following rating system to rate each employee: Exemplary, Good, Average, and Below Average. Amala Singh and Lien Ngyuen both received the same overall review of Average, and each employee responded differently to the assessment.

Read the passage. Then circle the letter of the answer to each question below the box.

Amala Singh was disappointed with the final assessment. She thought she had been doing a better job than Average. However, she accepted that her boss had reviewed several instances where her work was insufficient. Amala decided to take several steps:

- talk to her boss about how she could improve her proficiency and productivity

- offer to help on an upcoming large publishing project and offer to work overtime if needed to get the job done

- try to make all her upcoming publishing projects not only on time but ahead of schedule if possible

- periodically meet with her boss to get feedback on her performance instead of waiting until the next performance review

Lien Ngyuen was happy with the final assessment. She thought she had been doing a good job and that Average was an acceptable review for any employee. Lien decided to take several steps:

- politely thank her boss for the review and let her boss know that she would work to continue to perform at this level

- continue to make sure her projects were completed on time

- come in on time, take the appropriate lunch breaks, and leave at the appropriate time

- wait for the next performance assessment review and hope it comes in Average

---

1. What can you tell about the character of Amala Singh based on her response to the review?

   A   She responds negatively to criticism.

   B   She is self-aware and motivated.

   C   She is not concerned about her performance assessment.

   D   She is not respectful of her boss's opinions.

2. What can you tell about the character of Lien Nguyen based on her response to the review?

   F   She believes in working harder than others.

   G   She responds negatively to criticism.

   H   She is respectful of her boss's opinions and is satisfied with an Average assessment.

   J   She believes in taking positive initiatives to improve.

Write for Work

You are a manager for Eaton Publishing Company, and Amala Singh is one of the editors you manage. She has accomplished all the goals she set for herself in her response to the performance review of Average she received. She is approaching her next performance review. Consider what review you will give her from the four rating categories and write in a notebook a performance review stating why she is receiving this rating.

 **Reading Extension**

Turn to "James Herman Banning: Pioneer Pilot" on page 73 of *Reading Basics Advanced Reader*. After you have read and/or listened to the article, answer the questions below.

Circle the letter of the answer to each question.

1. Based on the article, what is one character trait you can say Banning possessed?

    A   resourcefulness

    B   laziness

    C   pessimism

    D   anger

2. What technique does the author use to reveal Bessie Coleman's character traits?

    F   inner thoughts

    G   action

    H   dialogue

    J   what other characters think about her

Write the answer to each question.

3. When the author writes, "Skeptics called them the *Flying Hobos*, a thinly veiled jab at the pair's lack of resources," what technique is the author using to reveal character traits?

   _____

   _____

4. In your opinion, what is the most prominent character trait Banning possesses? Why?

   _____

   _____

Explore Words

Write for Work

ANALOGIES

An analogy describes a relationship between two pairs of words. Analogies include a symbol (:) that stands for "is to" or "are to." Read this analogy:

Days : *week* as *minutes* : *hour*.

To complete an analogy, you need to figure out the relationship between the two words. In the example, the first word in each pair represents part of the second word; days are part of a week and minutes are part of an hour. Here are two other common kinds of analogies:

- Grammatical: *Man* : *men* as *mouse* : *mice*. The first word in each pair is a singular noun. The second word in each pair is plural.

- Object/Place: *Bed* : *bedroom* as *stove* : *kitchen*. Both pairs of words tell where an object is commonly found. A bed is found in a bedroom; a stove is found in a kitchen.

Choose a word from the box to complete each analogy. Write the word on the line.

loaf	preview	waist
genes	children	stable

1. *Glove* : *hand* as *belt* : _____.

2. *Write* : *right* as *jeans* : _____.

3. *Card* : *deck* as *slice* : _____.

4. *Teen* : *preteen* as *view* : _____.

5. *Car* : *garage* as *horse* : _____.

6. *Half* : *halves* as *child* : _____.

WORD FAMILIES

Words that have the same base word or root belong to the same word family. For example, the words *instruct*, *destruction*, and *structure* are in the same word family. They come from the root *struct*.

Circle the word in each row that does NOT belong to the word family.

1. courage	encouraging	courted	discouraged
2. supportive	transportation	reportable	sportsman
3. secular	perspective	spectacular	inspections

When you read, you will come across some unfamiliar words. You can often figure out their meaning by using context. Context means the words, phrases, and sentences that surround the unfamiliar word and give you clues to the word's meaning.

Read the passage. Pay attention to the underlined words.

> In 1974 Richard Nixon left his position as president of the United States. He <u>resigned</u> due to <u>controversy</u> over illegal activities that occurred during his campaign. Members of his staff were convicted of burglarizing the offices of the Democratic National Party. They were found guilty of planting electronic <u>surveillance</u> devices in order to record information to use against their opponents. The president denied any connection with the <u>alleged</u> break-in, although tapes later proved that he was involved.

Match each word on the left with its meaning on the right. Write the letter of the meaning next to the word. Use the context clues in the passage to help you.

_____ **1.** resigned   **a.** continual observation

_____ **2.** controversy   **b.** stepped down

_____ **3.** surveillance   **c.** disagreement

_____ **4.** alleged   **d.** believed, but not proven

Knowing these high-frequency words will help you in many school subjects.

characters   the people in a fictional work, such as a novel or story

traits   the things about people that make them special

encounter   to meet by chance

key   very important

technique   a way of doing something

Complete the sentences below using one of the words above.

1. The _____ feature of the room was the oversized skylight.

2. The main _____ in the book series are detectives.

3. I hope we _____ some interesting people on the trip.

4. Habitual lateness is one of Monifa's most annoying _____.

5. The _____ that the chef used to cook the fish was very complicated.

Lesson 2.6

Identify Style Techniques

Style techniques are ways of using language or the ways writers express themselves. Writers use many techniques to convey style in their writing. Good writers choose specific words to communicate moods, making readers feel sad, angry, or amused. Some words are used to persuade, while others simply provide information.

An element of style, or style technique, is the use of imagery. An image can appeal to any of the five senses. It makes readers imagine that they can see, hear, touch, taste, or smell what the writer is describing. Read the example and notice the images.

> Carlotta tipped the cup toward herself, inhaling the sharp bitter aroma, and felt steam on her mouth moments before the scalding coffee burned the skin on her tongue.

Another element of style is figurative language. One form of figurative language is a simile, which is a comparison using the word *like* or *as*. In a metaphor, a comparison is not stated but implied, and *like* or *as* is not used. A third kind of figurative language is personification, in which an animal or an inanimate object is compared to a human. Personification can be direct or implied. Read the examples of figurative language.

Simile: The new sports car looked like a spaceship.

Metaphor: The new sports car was a sleek spaceship.

Overt personification: The building was a friendly soldier, guarding the neighborhood.

Implied personification: We live beneath towering smokestacks, whose fierce breath once blackened the city.

In the last example, the "breath" of the smokestacks implies that they are alive.

Read the passage. What is the most prominent style technique used to create the mood?

> Only the scrape of our boots against rock and loose pebbles broke the silence as we moved deeper into the cave. Breathing had become an effort. The air, long stagnant from being kept in this tomblike cave, burned our throats and left a rancid taste. Foul-smelling and heavy, it seemed to stick in our lungs after each intake of breath.

The writer has chosen imagery as the main technique. In the first sentence, the writer describes the silent nature of the cave, broken only by the scrape of boots against rock. Later, words such as *stagnant*, *rancid*, and *foul-smelling* help the reader imagine the unpleasant atmosphere of the cave.

Read each sentence or passage. Then circle the letter of the answer to each question.

> The phone was a bird, chirping now and again, whose high call pierced the eardrums of all who heard it.

1. What figure of speech is used in this sentence?

   A   simile

   B   metaphor

> The asteroids were like tiny unnamed islands lost in the vast black void of space.

2. What figure of speech is used in this sentence?

   F   simile

   G   personification

> Malik slammed the brakes on the car and flung one arm sideways to protect Shalisa. The seatbelt dug into his shoulder, but he kept his grip on the wheel. The car slid onto the dewy grass, turning once, twice, three times before stopping.

3. What main style technique is used in this passage?

   A   imagery

   B   metaphor

> When I stepped outside, the Texas sun had just poked its nose over the horizon. The heat radiated off the asphalt, visible in waves to the naked eye.

4. The first sentence is an example of

   F   metaphor.

   G   personification.

> Every year the Adams River becomes a frothing maelstrom of flashing, jumping, twisting red sockeye as thousands of salmon arrive to spawn and die.

5. This sentence is an example of

   A   imagery.

   B   simile.

Read each passage. Then write the name of the sense or senses to which the imagery mainly appeals: *sight, sound, touch, taste,* or *smell*.

1. In the distance I saw a lighthouse silhouetted against the gray dawn.

   _____

2. From the shore bluffs you can hear the cry of the oyster-catcher and the hiss and rumble of surf over pebbles.

   _____

3. The thick, sweet scent of malt hung in the air for blocks around the brewery.

   _____

4. Almost everything tasted better when I was a kid. Now everything looks great but tastes like cardboard.

   _____

5. When Leah smiled, her amber eyes shone like a warm fire.

   _____

6. The odor coming from the swamp water reminded her of the stench of decayed leaves in the late fall.

   _____

7. The cedar-wood smell of pencil shavings mingled with the musty odor of the wet windowsill.

   _____

8. The days came in, cool and crisp, warmed to a pleasant slowness, and chilled again.

   _____

9. Javier let the chocolate melt on his tongue, its sweet taste in contrast to the cool mint that hid inside the candy shell.

   _____

10. The rough weave of the fabric scratched Isobel's arms. She tried to keep still so the itchy wool wouldn't rub against her skin any more than it had to.

   _____

Read each passage. Then circle the letter of the answer to each question.

There were 10 children in the group, each in the process of stripping off scarves and hats while the teacher's back was turned. Behind the children, their discarded gloves dotted the path, small piles of bright colors like fallen leaves. The day was unusually warm for March, and the sun beamed down, warming the children under their layers of warm clothes. Their teacher led them through the garden, pointing to the small stems, where flowers lay sleeping, waiting to wake up and bloom in the spring.

1. The phrase "small piles of bright colors like fallen leaves" is an example of what figure of speech?

   A metaphor

   B personification

   C simile

   D imagery

2. Which phrase in the passage is an image that appeals to the sense of touch?

   F "... waiting to wake up and bloom in the spring."

   G "... each in the process of stripping off scarves and hats while the teacher's back was turned."

   H "... their discarded gloves dotted the path ..."

   J "... the sun beamed down, warming the children under their layers of warm clothes."

The black snow lay in dirty heaps on the side of the road. What had looked so clean and beautiful as it fell now stood like a wall of frozen sludge lining the sidewalks, hard as brick in some places. For weeks, it sat there, slowly melting, every day getting filthier, taunting residents with the depressing thought, "It will never be spring."

3. To which sense does the image in the first sentence appeal?

   A sight

   B smell

   C touch

   D taste

4. "Taunting residents with the depressing thought, 'It will never be spring...'" is an example of what figure of speech?

   F metaphor

   G simile

   H personification

   J imagery

5. The phrase "now stood like a wall of frozen sludge" is an example of which figure of speech?

   A metaphor

   B simile

   C personification

   D imagery

6. Which phrase in the passage is an image that appeals to the sense of touch?

   F "... every day getting filthier."

   G "... black snow lay in dirty heaps ..."

   H "What had looked so clean and beautiful as it fell ..."

   J "... hard as brick in some places ..."

Workplace Skill:
Understand Style Techniques in Business Ads

Business owners use ads to convince customers to buy or use their products or services. Writers of effective business ads want to catch people's attention. Word choice and sentence structure are important tools in creating ads that appeal to customers to help a business reach its targeted audience.

Read the business ads. Then circle the letter of the answer to each question below the advertisements.

WILL TRUWHITE GIVE YOU THE BRIGHTEST SMILE?

Your smile says a lot about you—that's why you want to have the brightest, whitest teeth. The shinier your smile, the more often you'll want to use it. We promise you a 100-watt smile!

TruWhite is the best, most effective tooth whitener available. It comes in a pen with a brush-on application. Simply brush the whitener on your teeth. The pen is convenient, mess-free, and easy to use. You should begin seeing results in just two days—not a long time to wait for a movie-star smile!

A NEW CLINICALLY PROVEN TEETH WHITENER

ShineBrite professional teeth whitening product contains the only two-step tooth whitening kit that effectively removes and prevents stains without teeth bleaching or expensive cosmetic teeth whitening. ShineBrite is unique among professional teeth whitening products because of our patented and clinically proven active ingredient, C-101, which was developed over years of research by doctors at a top university. C-101 holds fast to teeth on a microscopic level by actually going under the surface of the stains to remove them evenly from teeth.

---

1. The two ads are similar in style because both

A use long, complex sentences.

B use short sentences and descriptive words.

C use persuasive language to convince customers.

D use a variety of punctuation to add visual impact.

2. What is the most likely reason the writer of the second ad used this writing style?

F She wanted the ad to sound professional and believable.

G She wanted the ad to sound casual and light-hearted.

H She wanted the ad to sound threatening and serious.

J She wanted the ad to sound informal and laid-back.

Write for Work

Your company has asked you to create an advertisement about an upcoming product—a computer game for 10- to 14-year-olds. Decide on the best word choice and style of writing to reach the targeted audience. Write the ad in a notebook.

 ## Workplace Extension

The Problem Situation

Raymond Chen has been working for the SS&G Accounting firm for 15 years as an accounting manager. He is an honest associate who is respected by all the clerks he supervises. Raymond is punctual and dependable, priding himself on providing monthly reports to his boss, the district account director, on schedule. This month's report is due by 10:00 A.M. Friday. It is already 9:30 A.M. on Friday, and Raymond is not receiving any cooperation from Rosalind Osei, who is to supply him with information he needs to complete the report. Rosalind also reports to the district account director. Raymond considers his options on how to best resolve the current situation.

Circle the letter of the answer to each question.

1. What would be Raymond's best course of action in this situation?

   A Raymond should speak directly and critically to Rosalind about the situation.

   B Raymond should calmly and clearly talk to his boss about the situation and ask for advice.

   C Raymond should compile the missing figures himself and boast that he did Rosalind's job.

   D Raymond should tell his boss that Rosalind needs to be fired.

2. Rosalind's actions show that in this particular situation she is

   F concerned about problem solving.

   G anxious to please her boss.

   H adequately meeting her deadlines.

   J a poor team player.

Write the answer to the question.

3. If you were confronted with this situation, what do you think the best course of action would be?

   _____

   _____

   _____

Explore Words

SYNONYMS

Words that have the same or almost the same meaning are synonyms. Some words that are synonyms have slightly different meanings. For example, *frugal* and *stingy* are synonyms, but look at these sentences:

> I learned how to be <u>frugal</u> when I lost my job.
>
> I learned how to be <u>stingy</u> when I lost my job.

The word *frugal* better fits the intended meaning of the sentence. *Frugal* means "economical," while *stingy* means "ungenerous."

Circle the word that better fits the meaning of each sentence.

1. He is very (proud, arrogant) about finally graduating from college.
2. Many people feel (frenzied, deranged) at holiday time.
3. Did you manage to (deceive, surprise) the kids with their presents?
4. Many parents have their kids (sanitize, clean) their own rooms.
5. My son is very (finicky, selective) when it comes to choosing friends.

PREFIXES *semi-, multi-, mid-*

A prefix is a word part that can be added to the beginning of many words. Adding a prefix changes the meaning of a word to which it is added. Here are some common prefixes, their meanings, and examples of words that include them:

semi-	"half of" or "partly"	*semicircle* (half of a circle)
multi-	"many"	*multicultural* (of many cultures)
mid-	"middle"	*midday* (the middle of the day)

Write a definition for each word below. Then write a short sentence using the word.

1. semiretired _____

_____

2. midtown _____

_____

3. multilevel _____

_____

LATIN ROOTS

Many English words have Latin roots. Knowing the meanings of roots can give you clues about the meanings of unfamiliar words. Here are the meanings of some common Latin roots.

sens, sent	"feel"	*clam, claim*	"shout" or "cry out"
rupt	"break"	*scrib, script*	"write"

Choose a word from the box to complete each sentence. Write the word and underline the Latin root.

resentment	sensitive	scribble	interrupt	subscribe	exclamation

1. An _____ point shows that a sentence should be read with strong emotion.

2. It's common to feel _____ when someone hurts your feelings.

3. Please do not _____ me while I am trying to work.

4. The baby loves to _____ with her crayons.

5. Do you _____ to any newspapers or magazines?

6. My _____ skin reacts badly to many soaps and lotions.

ACADEMIC VOCABULARY

Knowing these high-frequency words will help you in many school subjects.

style	a way of using language
specific	clearly defined or identified
communicate	to tell either by speaking or writing
element	a feature or aspect of something
figurative	metaphorical, not literal

Complete the sentences below using one of the words above.

1. Metaphor is one type of _____ language.

2. Hemingway wrote in a spare, clipped _____.

3. There are many ways to _____ with other people, including letters and e-mail.

4. Nizhoni couldn't think of a _____ reason that she'd lost the match.

5. One _____ of the novel that stood out was the use of short chapters.

Unit 2 Review

Identify Sequence

The order in which events take place is called sequence. When you read, it is important to understand how events, concepts, and themes relate to one another. Look for clue words that signal time order, such as *first*, *before*, *next*, *after*, *last*, and *then*. You also need to understand sequence to correctly follow directions.

Understand Consumer Materials

We are all consumers of both products and services. As consumers, we use materials, such as advertisements, coupons, product labels, instructions, and service forms and contracts. These materials contain important information for using or maintaining the products and services.

Use Reference Sources

The library and the Internet are filled with reference sources that give you important information about almost any topic. Some online sources are reliable, but many are not. It is important to know how to access the information and to evaluate sources for their reliability.

Use Supporting Evidence

When writers express an opinion or a main idea in writing, they must support it with evidence. Supporting evidence can be examples, facts, and statistics. Evaluating the evidence—deciding which evidence supports the main idea and which does not—helps you decide whether the writer's opinion or generalization is valid.

Recognize Character Traits

People in real life and characters in novels have character traits—ways of behaving, beliefs, physical characteristics, and patterns of speech. Fiction writers use narration, dialogue, and action to show character traits. Writers of nonfiction use some of these techniques to describe real people.

Identify Style Techniques

Authors use style techniques such as sentence structure, word choice, imagery, and figurative language to contribute to meaning. These techniques may emphasize persuasive points, help the reader imagine what is being described, or create a mood.

Unit 2 Assessment

Read each passage. Then circle the letter of the answer to each question.

> (1) Feeling lonelier than he'd ever felt in his 23 years on Earth, he let his book drop to the floor and rolled over to face the wall. (2) He heard sleet assaulting the window glass and the screech of truck brakes at the corner. (3) He thought of his brother, who had left home a soldier and had returned an invalid. (4) He thought of his own luckless life, of the father who walked out on his family and his mother's disappointments and growing detachment. (5) Unable to clear his head of the dark, persistent thoughts that swirled there like a growing storm, he closed his eyes and wished for sleep.

1. Which of the following words does NOT describe the character?

   A sad

   B bored

   C tormented

   D despairing

2. Which sentence in the passage is an image that appeals to the sense of hearing?

   F sentence 1

   G sentence 2

   H sentence 3

   J sentence 5

> For several decades in the 16th century, Spain was perhaps the most powerful country in the world. The days of Spain's glory began in 1492, when King Ferdinand and Queen Isabella sponsored Christopher Columbus's round-the-world voyage. After Columbus stumbled upon the Americas, Spanish explorers made huge claims of land in the New World. By 1550 Spain controlled Mexico, Central America, nearly all the islands of the West Indies, part of what is now the southwestern United States, and much of South America. At the same time, Spain also seized territories in what is now southern France, Italy, the Canary Islands, and parts of northern Africa. By the late 1500s, Spain also claimed lands in the Philippines. Until the failure of the Spanish Armada to conquer England in 1588, Spain was called the "mistress of the world and the queen of the ocean."

3. When did Spain first claim land in the Philippines?

   A when Columbus stumbled upon the Americas

   B before Spain controlled much of South America

   C right after King Ferdinand and Queen Isabella sponsored Columbus

   D after it claimed and controlled lands in the New World

4. Which reference source would you use to find out more information about 16th-century Spain?

   F a world almanac

   G a thesaurus

   H an atlas

   J an encyclopedia

Throughout history, people have invented clever devices to catch mice because of the terrible property damage that they can inflict. Although mice are quite clever, most mousetraps do the job they are meant to do. An early type of mousetrap was a simple device that dropped a heavy rock on the mouse when it touched the bait. One type of trap looks like a small prison with bars at the side of a small door. When a mouse wanders in, its weight causes a door to spring shut. Another kind of trap has a one-way door held shut by a weak spring. The mouse can get inside by pushing the door with its head, but once inside, the mouse can't get out. The most common trap is a small piece of wood with a spring in the center that snaps a wire across the mouse's neck.

5. Which sentence states the main idea of the passage?

A Throughout history, people have invented clever devices to catch mice because of the terrible property damage that they can inflict.

B Although mice are quite clever, most mousetraps do the job they are meant to do.

C One type of trap looks like a small prison with bars at the side of a small door.

D Another kind of trap has a one-way door held shut by a weak spring.

6. What kind of evidence does the writer use to support the main idea?

F descriptions of the lives of mousetrap inventors

G statistics about property damage caused by mice

H examples of several types of mousetraps

J facts about the chronological development of mousetrap technology

After Abraham Lincoln signed the Emancipation Proclamation, many Americans resented his freeing the slaves. Some let their wrath be known, even in the White House itself. An ugly occurrence took place at Lincoln's inaugural ball in 1865. The president had invited his friend Frederick Douglass, a former enslaved man famous for his writings and lectures, to the celebration. Douglass was the president's guest, but no one would let the African American man enter, not even the police who were guarding the White House. Douglass asked another guest to give Lincoln the message that he had arrived. In less than a minute, Douglass was invited into the room. Mr. Lincoln's face lit up as he said, "Here comes my friend Douglass."

7. Which of the following events happened first?

A the signing of the Emancipation Proclamation

B the freeing of slaves

C Douglass arriving at the inaugural ball

D Douglass being invited to the inaugural ball

8. Based on this passage, which character traits would you use to describe Lincoln?

F cautious and indecisive

G determined and unafraid

H trusting and thoughtful

J industrious and obedient

Michel de Notredame, known today as Nostradamus, lived in the 16th century. Nostradamus, a French astrologer and physician, seems to have possessed extraordinary powers of prediction. In a book called *Centuries*, he predicted several important events that would later take place. He predicted the French Revolution, the career of a man who may have been Napoleon, and the dates of royal births and deaths. He gained his greatest renown in Europe when he predicted the futures of the children of Catherine de Médicis. Because of Nostradamus's cryptic writing style, his predictions are subject to interpretation and debate.

9. Which sentence states the main idea of the passage?

A Michel de Notredame, known today as Nostradamus, lived in the 16th century.

B Because of Nostradamus's cryptic writing style, his predictions are subject to interpretation and debate.

C Nostradamus, a French astrologer and physician, seems to have possessed extraordinary powers of prediction.

D He gained his greatest renown in Europe when he predicted the futures of the children of Catherine de Médicis.

10. Which sentence could be added to the paragraph to act as additional supporting evidence for the main idea?

F Nostradamus was born on December 14, 1503.

G Nostradamus was court physician to King Charles IX of France.

H Nostradamus predicted the rise of a dictator in Germany in the 1930s.

J Nostradamus is known for his innovative medical treatments during outbreaks of the plague.

Read the chart. Then circle the letter of the answer to each question.

MP3 Players					
○ Excellent		◑ Good	⊖ Fair	● Poor	
Brand/Model	Price	Headphones	Problem Disks	Bumps	Features
Smith E54	$89	◑	⊖	⊖	⊖
Tunes 25	$99	⊖	⊖	●	●
ABX 162	$130	○	◑	●	●
LectraSound AB30	$125	◑	○	◑	○

11. Which MP3 player has the highest rating for features?

A Smith E54

B Tunes 25

C ABX 162

D LectraSound AB30

12. If the lowest price was the most important consideration, which MP3 player would you buy?

F Smith E54

G Tunes 25

H ABX 162

J LectraSound AB30

Read this cover letter to a prospective employer. Then circle the letter of the answer to each question.

322 West Main Street
Attleboro, MA 02703
November 2

Tai Chen
Manager, Chez Laurent
4 Stanton Street
Boston, MA 02215
(512) 555-3909

Dear Ms. Chen,

I found your advertisement for a hostess in our local newspaper, and I am looking for just such a job. I believe that my qualifications very closely meet the needs outlined in your advertisement. Your restaurant has an excellent reputation for both its food and service, and I am very interested in working in a position that will utilize my skills and experience.

I have extensive work experience as a member of the wait staff at Jacqueline's Bistro, an upscale restaurant in Providence, Rhode Island. In my current position there, I am responsible for waiting on dinner guests. I also help out answering calls and making reservations. At my previous job, I operated the cash register, processing both cash and credit-card transactions. I am very enthusiastic and career-minded and have excellent communication and mathematics skills. My enclosed résumé lists my other skills, qualifications, and professional experience.

Please review my résumé and contact me to set up an interview at your earliest convenience if you think that I am a qualified candidate. I look forward to hearing from you.

Thank you for your time and consideration.

Sincerely,

Amalia Morales

13. Which sentence could be added to the second paragraph of the letter to act as additional supporting evidence for the main idea?

   A   I enjoy reading and am an avid bridge player.

   B   I am able to remain calm and courteous during rush periods and always resolve customer problems in a satisfactory manner.

   C   I have a daughter in third grade, a son in kindergarten, and another child on the way.

   D   I can start work any time after the first of the year.

14. What elements characterize the writing style of the letter?

   F   long sentences and precise, professional language

   G   short sentences and casual language

   H   similes and metaphors

   J   imagery that helps the reader see what is being described

Read a portion of Amalia Morales's résumé. Then circle the letter of the answer to each question.

Summary of Qualifications

- Five years experience in the restaurant industry
- Strong communication, problem-solving, and customer-service skills
- College-level classes in business, math, bookkeeping, and consumer science

Special Skills

- Proficient in point-of-sale software applications
- Proficient in Spanish
- Some knowledge of Portugese

Work Experience

2010–present: Wait Staff, Jacqueline's Bistro, Providence, Rhode Island

- Wait tables during high-volume dinner service
- Suggested new procedure to streamline scheduling
- Direct and coordinate bussing staff
- Make telephone reservations for customers
- Answer telephone questions regarding restaurant hours, menu items, and directions

2006–2010: Cashier, Corner Deli, Portland, Maine

- Accurately rung up cash and credit-card transactions in a busy neighborhood restaurant
- Took telephone and fax orders for customer pickup
- Excellent organizational, customer-service, and math skills

Education

2005: Attended online training classes in alcohol safe service

2005–2006: Audited courses in business, math, bookkeeping, and consumer science at Downeast Community College, Portland, Maine

2004: Graduated from Newsom High School, York, Maine

---

15. When did Morales take classes at a community college?

- A after she worked at Corner Deli
- B before she graduated from high school
- C after she graduated from high school
- D while she worked for Jacqueline's Bistro

16. What can you conclude about Morales's character from her résumé and cover letter?

- F She has an unrealistically high opinion of herself.
- G She is basically insecure.
- H She is responsible and hardworking.
- J She is an ambitious but lazy employee.

Circle the letter of the answer to each question.

17. Which word does NOT belong to the same word family?

    A memorize

    B demonstrate

    C remember

    D memorial

18. Which analogy is correct?

    F *Glass* : *window* as *brick* : *kitchen*.

    G *Glass* : *window* as *brick* : *chimney*.

    H *Glass* : *window* as *brick* : *foundry*.

    J *Glass* : *window* as *brick* : *hard*.

19. Which is the correct meaning of *humorous*?

    A the opposite of humor

    B not at all funny

    C characterized by humor

    D partly funny

20. Which two words share the same Latin root?

    F exclaim, excite

    G interrupt, disruption

    H sensitive, sending

    J scripture, rupture

21. Which is the correct meaning of *multicultural*?

    A being cultured

    B partly cultured

    C the opposite of cultured

    D relating to many cultures

22. Which word means "the study of Earth"?

    F phonology

    G biology

    H geology

    J zoology

23. Which group of words are synonyms?

    A modest, flattered, embarrassed

    B forgive, blame, punish

    C approximately, exactly, almost

    D clarify, illustrate, explain

24. Which word means "people who write together"?

    F subwriters

    G cowriters

    H prewriters

    J rewriters

25. Which of these represents the correct division and accent of the word *repeal*?

    A re **peal**

    B rep **eal**

    C re peal

    D rep eal

26. Which is NOT a meaning of the word *step*?

    F to block or close up a hole or leak

    G one action in a series of instructions

    H to move one's foot in order to walk

    J one of the flat parts of a staircase

27. Which two words are homophones?

    A Sunday, Monday

    B ask, answer

    C patients, patience

    D thankful, grateful

28. Which word means "the result of polluting"?

    F polluter

    G polluted

    H pollute

    J pollution

29. Which word means "to make tangled"?

    A untangle

    B entangle

    C tangled

    D tangly

Unit 3

In this unit you will learn how to

You will practice the following workplace skills

You will also learn new words and their meanings and put your reading skills to work in written activities. You will get additional reading practice in *Reading Basics Advanced Reader*.

Lesson 3.1

Make Generalizations

Generalizations are statements that apply to many people, facts, events, or situations. They can be conclusions drawn from what has been said, or they can introduce more specific information that will follow. Writers sometimes utilize signal words to introduce a generalization, and they can include *most, many, few, all, usually, generally*, and *typically*. However, not all generalizations include a signal word.

When you make generalizations, you should call on the skills you learned from drawing conclusions. Both skills require the reader to examine the text and come to a conclusion. Every generalization is a conclusion, but not every conclusion is a generalization. Conclusions can be general or specific, but when you make a generalization, you come to a broad conclusion based on several pieces of evidence. Read the example:

> Seaweed is eaten by people worldwide because of its vitamin and mineral content. Substances that are produced from seaweed include algin, agar, and carrageenan. Carrageenan is added to many products that people use every day, including toothpaste and paper. Algin is used in soap and paint, and it is the base that scientists often use when they grow bacteria.

The passage provides examples about specific uses of seaweed by people and companies. From this, the reader can make the generalization that seaweed has many different uses. This is a valid generalization—it is based on information in the passage, and it makes sense. Not all generalizations are valid, however. If, for example, you made the generalization that seaweed is mostly used as food, it would not be valid. The passage gives examples of seaweed being eaten, but it also talks about seaweed being used for other purposes. The information in the passage does not support that generalization, so it is not valid.

Read the passage. Then make a valid generalization.

> Some bacteria are essential to the growth of plants, and some are valuable decomposers. They break down dead tissue so that dead plants and animals don't litter Earth. This process adds nutrients to the soil, which Earth's plant life needs to thrive. Some bacteria cause food to spoil, while others cause diseases, such as strep throat and tuberculosis. Without antibiotics, many people could die from these diseases.

The passage gives specific examples of things bacteria can do. A valid generalization is that bacteria can cause many different things to happen. Another valid generalization is that bacteria can help to both create growth and break down matter.

Read each passage. Then circle the letter of the most valid generalization based on the information in each passage.

> Most desert animals are active at night when the temperature is cooler. Many of the plants that live in the desert, such as the cactus, store large amounts of water in their roots or stems. Some desert plants have deep roots, and other plants have tiny leaves or a waxy covering to reduce water loss from evaporation.

1. A Deserts get very little rain.

   B All desert plants store water in their roots or stems.

   C Desert plants and animals are adapted to harsh, dry conditions.

   D Desert animals rarely see the sun.

> The power of glaciers is evident in the mountains and canyons that have been shaped by ages of glacial movement. Many mountains have had their heights increased by glaciers, though in other parts of the world, melting glaciers have led to the erosion of mountains. The Great Lakes are also a product of their handiwork, having been formed by the melting of mile-thick glaciers.

2. F Ice is destructive.

   G Mountains were formed by many different forces.

   H Glaciers were active in North America for thousands of years.

   J Glaciers are both a destructive and a creative force.

> Many of the commonly accepted tips for distinguishing a poisonous mushroom from a nonpoisonous mushroom are false. For instance, there are no consistent markings that can be used to tell the two apart. A safe mushroom growing in one area might look just like a poisonous one found elsewhere. Many people believe that all mushrooms that grow on wood are safe to eat, but this is simply untrue.

3. A Experienced mushroom hunters can tell the difference between poisonous and edible mushrooms.

   B People should not eat mushrooms that grow in the wild because they may be poisonous.

   C Poisonous mushrooms look very different from edible mushrooms.

   D The safest policy is to avoid eating mushrooms altogether.

Read each passage. Then write a valid generalization based on the details in the passage.

Anise is a member of the parsley family along with dill, caraway, coriander, parsnips, and fennel. Anise tastes like licorice and is used to flavor everything from cake to cheese to meats and fish. A long time ago, Europeans used anise to treat epilepsy and as a charm to prevent nightmares. Those traditions are long gone, but anise is still used for medicinal purposes. It is often used in cough drops and syrups and to soothe colicky babies.

1. _____

_____

Many people know the folk song about John Henry's race against a steam drill. Not everyone knows that John Henry was a real person who actually raced a drill. The real John Henry is said to have been killed by a falling rock, however, not by exhaustion. Johnny Appleseed is based on John Chapman, who was born in Massachusetts during the Revolutionary War. There are fact-based stories about Chapman planting orchards across Ohio and Indiana, but descriptions of his eccentric clothes and odd behavior may be greatly exaggerated.

2. _____

_____

_____

The discovery of gold in California in 1848 created an intense demand for a transportation link across Panama to connect the Atlantic and Pacific Oceans. In 1855 a railroad line was completed after years of hard labor in the swamps and jungles. During its construction, workers died from yellow fever and malaria. In 1881 a French organization tried to build a canal across the isthmus, but again, workers struggled mightily against heat and disease. Many workers died before the French gave up their attempts to build the canal in 1889.

3. _____

_____

_____

Read each passage. Then circle the letter of the answer to each question.

> Dizziness, at its worst, is the sensation that the world is spinning around you. Heart problems and high or low blood pressure can cause dizziness. Losing too much blood because of disease or injury can also be a cause. Some other causes of dizziness include brain tumors, epilepsy, and other diseases that affect the brain. Some infections and fevers can cause temporary dizziness. Dizzy spells can even be caused by too much earwax or by getting new eyeglasses.

1. The details in this passage

   A   are mainly about heart and blood problems.

   B   are mainly about the effects of dizzy spells.

   C   are mainly about causes of dizziness.

   D   are mainly about measures to prevent dizziness.

2. What generalization can you make from the details in this passage?

   F   Dizziness sometimes has a serious underlying cause.

   G   All causes of dizziness come from medical problems.

   H   Most causes of dizziness are unknown.

   J   Dizziness is usually temporary.

> After the Civil War, industries in America grew. The national railroad system greatly expanded, and with the invention of the telegraph, nationwide communication was established. The invention of new processing techniques led to the creation of a giant steel industry. New coalfields opened, and oil-well drilling developed. An electrical generator capable of delivering the large amount of power needed for industry was then invented.

3. The details in this passage

   A   are mainly about the Civil War.

   B   are mainly about electrical generators.

   C   are mainly about the growth of new industries.

   D   are mainly about improvements in communications.

4. What generalization can you make from the details in this passage?

   F   New inventions had little impact on people's lives.

   G   New inventions helped many new industries to grow.

   H   New inventions only succeeded in expanding the railroad industry.

   J   New inventions were mainly focused on individuals.

Workplace Skill:
Make Generalizations about Sections of an Employee Handbook

You can make generalizations about information in memos, handbooks, and other communications. Decide how the generalized information applies to your job.

Read the following sections of an employee handbook. Then circle the letter of the answer to each question below the box.

Section 4: Company Dress Code

On Monday through Thursday, attire is business casual. Casual attire is permitted on Friday. Please note the following points:

- Trendy items should be carfeully considered, as they may not be appropriate.
- Everyone should present himself or herself with clean, neat clothing and good grooming.
- Women should avoid excessively short skirts.
- T-shirts should be avoided unless worn under a jacket or sweater.
- Jeans, sandals, and sneakers are only allowed on Fridays.
- Flip-flops are never allowed in the office.

Section 5: Computer Usage

- All resources, applications, and programs that you need for your project should be available to you. If you are missing anything you need, please make a request to your director.
- Do not alter your computer in any way. Do not download software, even if it is necessary for your project. Ask the system administrator to provide you with the software you require.
- Personal e-mail should not be sent from your work account, and you should not check your personal account from your company computer.
- Do not store personal photos, documents, or MP3 files on your company computer.
- Others may access your computer if you are not here. Keep files clearly organized.

---

1. Which of the following generalizations can you make, based on section 4?

- **A** It is acceptable to wear any trendy clothing to the office.
- **B** The office dress code is formal attire.
- **C** Flip-flops are allowed, but only on Fridays.
- **D** Everyone should always wear clean, neat clothing, even on Fridays.

2. Which of the following generalizations can you make, based on section 5?

- **F** Do not store any files on your company computer.
- **G** You can use your company computer as an extra personal computer.
- **H** Use your company computer only for work purposes.
- **J** Do not to send too many e-mails while at work.

Write for Work

At the company staff meeting, employees are asked to give short presentations about different company policies and procedures. You have been asked to give a presentation about one of the handbook sections that describe the dress code policy or the computer usage policy. In a notebook, write a short presentation of two to four sentences to convey the most important parts of one of the policies. Then sum up your presentation with generalizations about how to appropriately dress or how to use your company computer appropriately.

 ## Reading Extension

Turn to "Embedded Journalists: Writing from the Front Lines" on page 81 of *Reading Basics Advanced Reader*. After you have read and/or listened to the article, answer the questions below.

Circle the letter of the answer to each question.

1. What generalization can you make about how journalists feel about the embedded journalist program?

   A   Journalists would rather be war correspondents than be embedded.

   B   Journalists feel that the embedded program is a positive experience.

   C   Journalists feel that the embedded program challenges their journalistic integrity.

   D   Journalists like the embedded program because it gives them the chance to write anti-war articles.

2. What generalization can you make about embedded journalists?

   F   Embedded journalists are always able to protect themselves while they are embedded.

   G   Embedded journalists always write stories that are objective.

   H   Embedded journalists are often in danger.

   J   Embedded journalists always abide by the embedding agreement.

3. What generalization can you make about the embedding agreement?

   A   It prevents journalists from writing the stories they want to write.

   B   It keeps journalists from the front lines.

   C   It tells journalists that they must write about battle preparations.

   D   It provides journalists with protection from the public.

Write the answer to the question.

4. What generalization can you make about war correspondents?

_____

_____

Explore Words

SYNONYMS AND ANTONYMS

Synonyms are words with the same, or almost the same, meaning. For example, *cold* and *frigid* are synonyms. Antonyms are words that have opposite meanings. For example, *cold* and *hot* are antonyms.

Write a synonym and an antonym for each word. Use a dictionary or thesaurus if necessary.

1. fortunate   _____   _____

2. damage   _____   _____

3. powerful   _____   _____

4. build   _____   _____

5. intelligent   _____   _____

6. reliable   _____   _____

7. bravery   _____   _____

8. cautious   _____   _____

ACCENTED AND UNACCENTED SYLLABLES

A syllable is a word part that has one vowel sound. In multisyllabic words, one of the syllables is accented, or stressed. Knowing syllable accent patterns can help you read and spell multisyllabic words.

- In three-syllable words, the accent is usually on the first syllable. The unaccented middle syllable usually has the schwa sound. The schwa sound is similar to the short *u* or short *i* sound. You can hear it in the second syllable of these words: hab/i/tat, mar/ma/lade, ac/ti/vate.

- In three-syllable words that include a prefix, a root, and a suffix or word ending, the accent is usually on the second syllable: in/vent/or, re/spect/ing, con/trac/tion.

Divide each word into syllables and circle the accented syllable. The first item has been done for you.

1. cel/e/brate   5. satisfied   9. unyielding

2. cinnamon   6. mistaken   10. simulate

3. disgusting   7. carefully   11. resisting

4. unsteady   8. overly   12. dangerous

SUFFIXES -ness, -ship

A suffix is a word part that can be added to the end of many words. Adding a suffix changes the meaning of the word to which it is added. The suffixes *-ness* and *-ship* mean "the state of being." Therefore, *happiness* is "the state of being happy," and *friendship* is "the state of being friends."

Write a word with the suffix *-ness* or *-ship* that has the meaning of each phrase.

1. the state of being alert _____

2. the state of being a champion _____

3. the state of being bitter _____

4. the state of being boastful _____

5. the state of being careless _____

6. the state of being a citizen _____

7. the state of being healthy _____

8. the state of being a partner _____

9. the state of being polite _____

ACADEMIC VOCABULARY

Knowing these high-frequency words will help you in many school subjects.

statement	a clear expression of something in speech or writing
apply	to be suitable or relevant
utilize	to make use of
valid	supporting the intended point or claim
essential	absolutely necessary

Complete the sentences below using one of the words above.

1. The manager made sure to _____ the company's key terms when she gave her presentation.

2. The president gave a _____ to the press.

3. In some states, the sales tax does not _____ to food or clothing.

4. Letting each coat of varnish dry is _____ to creating a smooth finish.

5. During the debate, the candidate was forced to admit that his opponent had a _____ point.

Lesson 3.2

Recognize Author's Effect and Intention

An author's intention is what he or she hopes the reader will take away after reading his or her text. To accomplish this, an author must decide on an approach toward the material, subject, and audience. Style techniques such as word choice, sentence structure, imagery, and figurative language create an effect, such as humor, sarcasm, excitement, anger, or suspense. For example, an author might use figurative language, such as similes, in order to create an effect of sarcasm. An author might also use formal language to create an authoritative effect, or he or she might use casual, informal language to create a friendly effect.

Read the example and note the way the author uses language:

> The wind howled past the window, setting the torn screen in the bedroom window flapping. The window frame shook, and Camilla thought it was likely to come off before the storm was over. Outside in the wilderness that surrounded the cabin, some creature cried out a primitive wail, protesting the storm. Camilla tightened the lock on the window with shaking hands and hoped that whatever foul beast was out there wouldn't come any closer.

In this passage, the author uses the words *howled, wilderness, primitive, wail,* and *foul* to create a sense of fright and suspense. Phrases such as *with shaking hands* and *foul beast* show Camilla's fear. The effect of the passage is suspense. The author's intention is to thrill the reader with a passage that is frightening or suspenseful.

Read the passage. Then identify the author's effect and intention.

> Astronomy was the first of my lasting loves, and it overtook me during the total eclipse of 1925. I was staggered by the "diamond ring" effect, caused by the last bit of the sun's face blazing between mountain peaks on the moon's edge. Then the total eclipse began, the stars came out, and I was thrilled. For years to come I would travel the world—India, South Africa, China—seeking another total eclipse to rekindle that first moment of awe.

From the passage, you can conclude that the author's intention is to convey his or her love of astronomy by describing what he or she saw during an eclipse. Words like *staggered, thrilled,* and *awe* help create an effect of wonder and excitement.

Read each passage. Then circle the letter of the answer to each question.

> The restaurant was overflowing with customers, and my assigned section was full of screaming children who were acting like overexcited zoo animals. I wasn't familiar with the menu yet and had even less understanding of the timing involved in serving food. I was scared that I would drop things, and I noticed that my hands were shaking like a leaf in the wind. None of the other wait staff had to write down their tables' orders, but I had a hard time remembering what people were ordering even moments after they spoke. I felt like everything people said to me was just leaking out of my brain. I brought risotto to a table that had ordered ravioli, and when the patron yelled at me, I burst into tears right in the middle of the restaurant, just like a little kid.

1. What effect is created by the writing style?

   A anxiety

   B a sense of comfort

2. Which best describes the author's intention?

   F to convey how annoying children can be

   G to convey the nerves he or she felt on his or her first night waiting tables

> I've worked for a veterinarian for several years. During that time, I've discovered that many people like only one kind of pet, and some people don't choose very well. Cat people believe that felines are superior to other animals, but it might just be that cats act superior and standoffish. Cat owners say that felines are very intelligent, even though there is simply no evidence to support this. A cat's greatest accomplishment may be that it gets its owners to feed it even after "decorating" the carpet with its fur and "improving" the furniture with its claws. Cats are low maintenance because they don't want—or allow—much attention. Dog people, on the other hand, are much more clear sighted about the merits of their pets. They believe that canines are friendlier than cats and that dogs are loyal and devoted to their humans. Dogs can learn tricks, which most cats can't or won't do, and dogs love to play fetch or run after a ball. Playing with dogs and walking them is good exercise for their owners as well.

3. What effect is created by the author's approach to the material?

   A excitement

   B sarcasm

4. Which best describes the author's intention?

   F to persuade the reader that dogs are better than cats

   G to give scientific facts about cats and dogs

Read each passage. Then write the answer to each question.

> Train travel may seem easy, but I promise that it is harder than it looks. It's not like flying, where someone is constantly checking your ticket at every turn. You better double-check your own train ticket before you get on because you're on your own until well after it has started moving. In Italy, I tried to go from Florence to Rome by train and didn't realize I was going the wrong way until I saw the Leaning Tower of Pisa out the window.

1. Does the author's style create a lighthearted or authoritative effect? _____

2. Based on the passage, what do you think the author's intention was for writing?

_____

> An English hostel (which is like a hotel but provides no services aside from a sleeping room) issued instructions to its guests through signs bearing unique messages. One sign, for instance, says, "Americans are requested to retire before 2:00 A.M." Another notice asks German visitors to stay in bed until at least 6:00 A.M. "Italians," a last sign read, "are requested to refrain from singing after 10:00 P.M."

3. Does the author's style create a serious or humorous effect? _____

4. Based on the passage, what do you think the author's intention was for writing?

_____

> Mountain climbing can provide you with a fresh look at the world around you. As you climb, your attention drifts away from everyday concerns to the challenges of moving forward. Pushed beyond your physical limits, you discover the power of determination and positive thinking. When you reach the top, you will be able to survey mountains, valleys, and the bigger world of which you are just a part.

5. Does the author's style create an effect of inspiration or negativity? _____

6. Based on the passage, what do you think the author's intention was for writing? _____

_____

Read each passage. Then circle the letter of the answer to each question.

> Over the years, scientists have considered several theories to explain how the moon formed. Some argued that the moon was captured by Earth's gravity, while others thought it formed from the same nebula as Earth. Today, evidence from the Apollo missions that were conducted in the 1960s and 1970s supports another explanation. Analysis of the moon rock collected during the Apollo missions shows that the moon is made of the same material as Earth's crust and mantle, with some exceptions. Unlike Earth, the moon has little or no iron. These facts suggest that the moon formed as a result of a giant impact with young Earth. The impact broke away a large amount of vaporized material, and it is thought that gravity pulled this material together to form the moon.

1. The effect of the author's language is a feeling of

   A authority.

   B humor.

   C anger.

   D suspense.

2. From this passage you can conclude that the author's intention is to

   F relate the successes of the first Apollo mission.

   G argue against further space exploration.

   H convince readers that more trips to the moon should be undertaken.

   J present a theory on the origins of the moon.

> International trade is based on the principle of mutual benefit, which means both parties in the exchange are better off after the exchange takes place than before. International trade also encourages each country to specialize in the production of goods best suited to its resources. When countries specialize, they use their resources more efficiently, and global output of goods and services increases. This benefits buyers and sellers in all trading countries. International trade helps create a more prosperous global economy.

3. The author uses language to create an effect that is

   A wary.

   B negative.

   C positive.

   D suspicious.

4. From this passage you can conclude that the author's intention is to

   F convince readers that international trade is beneficial.

   G present reasons why international trade is bad for some nations.

   H outline a plan to make international trade more effective.

   J give a balanced view of the benefits and drawbacks of international trade.

Workplace Skill: Understand Author's Effect and Intention in a Cover Letter

At work, you may need to determine the author's intention for writing documents such as policy statements, memos, and letters. To understand the author's intention, ask yourself what the author wants to accomplish with this document. Then determine what effect you think he or she is trying to create. Word choice and language are important in creating the effect the author wants to achieve.

Read the cover letter for a position as a nurse assistant. Then circle the letter of the answer to each question below the box.

Dear Ms. Moreno:

In response to your recent advertisement in the *Chicago Sun-Times*, I am writing to express my interest in the nurse assistant position currently available at Sunny Days Senior Home.

As the attached résumé further details, I have extensive experience in the health care field. I have held positions as a nurse assistant at hospitals, outpatient centers, and doctors' offices. I believe this field experience, as well as my Nurse Assistant Certification, would make me a valuable candidate for the position at Sunny Days Senior Home. In addition to practical experience and education, I have a strong work ethic, a cooperative attitude, team spirit, and a desire to help others, which I believe would make me an exemplary staff member.

I would appreciate the opportunity to discuss my qualifications with you at a mutually convenient time. Thank you in advance for your time and consideration, and I look forward to speaking with you.

Respectfully yours,

Rima Freeman

Enclosure: résumé

1. What effect does the writing style convey to someone reading the letter?

   A uncertainty and indecisiveness

   B informality and casualness

   C professionalism and formality

   D friendliness and approachability

2. What do you think the author's intention was for writing?

   F to give information about how to become a nurse assistant

   G to convince Ms. Moreno that she has the qualifications for the position

   H to inspire others to apply for the nurse assistant position

   J to use her superior letter-writing abilities

Write for Work

Imagine you are Rima Freeman and Ms. Moreno granted you an interview for the position of nurse assistant. In a notebook, write or e-mail Ms. Moreno a letter thanking her for the interview. Be sure to include specific details, reasons, and examples that will remind Ms. Moreno why you are the best person for the job. Express your enthusiasm about the opportunity to work at Sunny Days Senior Home.

 Reading Extension

Turn to "Bush Pilots: Tough Takeoffs, Rough Landings" on page 89 of *Reading Basics Advanced Reader*. After you have read and/or listened to the article, answer the questions below.

Circle the letter of the answer to each question.

1. What effect is created by the author's use of the quotation at the beginning of the article?

    A   authority

    B   lightheartedness

    C   anger

    D   spookiness

2. What is the author's intention for writing this article?

    F   to illustrate that bush pilots are always silly

    G   to convince the reader to become a bush pilot

    H   to convey the fearlessness of bush pilots

    J   to show the reader that bush pilots are irresponsible

3. What effect do you think the author intended to create by including the story about pizza in paragraph 4?

    A   playfulness

    B   spookiness

    C   terror

    D   excitement

4. Read paragraphs 7 and 8. What effect is created by these paragraphs?

    F   humor

    G   frustration

    H   respect

    J   despair

Write the answer to each question.

5. What words does the author use to create the effect in paragraphs 7 and 8?

    _____

    _____

6. What do you think the author's intention was for including Heather Stewart's story?

    _____

    _____

Explore Words

Write for Work

GREEK ROOTS

Many English words have Greek roots. Knowing the meaning of common Greek roots can help you figure out what an unfamiliar word means.

chron	"time"	**therm**	"heat"
ast	"star"	*man*	"hand"

Use what you know about roots to match each word in the first column with its definition in the second column. Write the matching letter on the line.

_____ **1.** manual   **a.** a container that maintains the temperature of something

_____ **2.** thermos   **b.** a person who travels to the stars

_____ **3.** chronic   **c.** the study of the stars and other objects in space

_____ **4.** manipulate   **d.** persisting for a long time

_____ **5.** chronological   **e.** done with the hands

_____ **6.** astronomy   **f.** in time order

_____ **7.** thermometer   **g.** to move with one's hands

_____ **8.** astronaut   **h.** a device for measuring temperature

SYNONYMS

Words that have the same or almost the same meaning are synonyms. Some words that are synonyms have slightly different meanings, however. For example, *unusual* and *bizarre* are synonyms, but read these sentences:

Your daughter's name is <u>unusual</u>.

Your daughter's name is <u>bizarre</u>.

The word *unusual* better fits the intended meaning of the sentence. *Unusual* means "uncommon," while *bizarre* means "strange."

Circle the word that better fits the meaning of each sentence.

1. I have always (prodded, encouraged) my son to play team sports.

2. My neighbor is lovely. She's so (chatty, long-winded) whenever we meet.

3. I think he was (misguided, mistaken) about whom he saw at the diner yesterday.

4. I admire that you are so (stubborn, strong-willed) at work.

5. Taking out the garbage is one of my son's (burdens, responsibilities).

SUFFIXES -al, -ial

A suffix is a word part that can be added to the end of many words. Adding a suffix changes the meaning of the word to which it is added. The suffixes -al and -ial mean "having the characteristics of" or "relating to." Therefore, *magical* means "having the characteristics of magic," and *adversarial* means "having the characteristics of an adversary."

Write a word with the suffix -al or -ial that has the meaning of each phrase.

1. having the characteristics of architecture _____

2. relating to politics _____

3. relating to education _____

4. having the characteristics of commerce _____

5. relating to music _____

6. having the characteristics of bacteria _____

7. having the characteristics of a ceremony _____

8. relating to a family _____

9. having the characteristics of a proverb _____

ACADEMIC VOCABULARY

Knowing these high-frequency words will help you in many school subjects.

approach   a way of dealing with something

intention   a goal or plan

convey   to communicate a message or information

constant   occurring continuously over a period of time

unique   unlike anything else

Complete the sentences below using one of the words above.

1. When the first plan didn't succeed, the team took a different _____ to the problem.

2. With round-the-clock shifts, the nurses kept a _____ watch on the patient.

3. It was Ming's _____ to go to the store before heading to class.

4. Carmen felt that her protest sign didn't really _____ how angry she was.

5. Each user of the company e-mail system must have a _____ ID.

Lesson 3.3

Compare and Contrast

Writers frequently use comparison and contrast to discuss two or more similar topics. You compare two or more things when you consider how they are alike, and you contrast them when you judge how they are different. Comparison and contrast are frequently employed in the same piece of writing.

Writers use these words and phrases as signals to show comparison and contrast.

Comparison	Contrast
also, likewise, alike,	although, however,
by comparison,	in contrast, on the contrary,
similarly	on the other hand

Read the example in which the writer compares and contrasts types of mixtures:

> A mixture is made of two or more kinds of matter that are mixed together but not chemically changed. A bowl of cereal, milk, and strawberries is a mixture. Likewise, a jar filled with nickels and dimes is also a mixture. These are heterogeneous mixtures, meaning they have distinct parts or regions. In contrast, stirring salt in water creates a homogeneous mixture. In this type of mixture, every part of it is the same.

In the example above, the words *likewise* and *also* indicate comparison. The phrase *in contrast* indicates contrast.

Read the passage. Note which items are being compared and contrasted.

Tokyo, which means "eastern capital," has been Japan's capital for more than a century, but before that, Kyoto was the great capital for over 1,000 years. Many parts of today's noisy Tokyo were rebuilt haphazardly after the city was bombed during World War II. Kyoto was also scheduled to be bombed, but U.S. Secretary of War Henry L. Stimson argued for its exclusion. Kyoto was spared, and it was the only major Japanese city to escape bombing during the war. Today, mellowed by 12 centuries, Kyoto has the grace of old silver. Kyoto is Japan's perfumed past, while Tokyo is Japan's dynamic present. Tokyo is her brain, but Kyoto is her soul.

The two items being compared and contrasted are Japan's current and former capitals. Tokyo and Kyoto are similar because they are both major cities in Japan that have served as the country's capital. The cities are different because Tokyo is noisy and dynamic, while Kyoto is mellow and graceful.

Read the passage. Then write the answers to the questions.

The Washington Monument was completed in 1884 and is located in Washington, D.C. The Tower of Pisa, on the other hand, was completed in the late 1300s and is in the old city of Pisa, Italy. The two buildings have one major feature in common. They are both the victims of unstable soil. As it was built, the weight of the 180-foot Tower of Pisa caused the building to settle into the unstable soil, causing the tower's famous lean. In the 20th century, the tower was still sinking 0.05 inches per year, and a major project was undertaken to keep the building from collapse. In comparison, the 555-foot Washington Monument had extensive subfoundations constructed in 1876, after it was discovered that the monument was unstable and sinking.

1. What two subjects are being compared and contrasted?

_____

_____

2. Name some ways in which the two subjects differ.

_____

_____

3. Name some ways in which the two subjects are alike.

_____

_____

4. What do the two buildings have in common concerning later construction?

_____

_____

5. What signal words and phrases does the writer use to indicate comparison?

_____

6. What signal words and phrases does the writer use to indicate contrast?

_____

Read the passage. Then complete the table.

If you are watching European football, you are seeing a different game than if you are watching American football. European football is the game that Americans know as soccer. Although American football developed in part from the European game, it changed a lot when it crossed the ocean. Soccer players kick a mostly round ball into a net goal to score one point. In contrast, American football players carry a pointed, oval ball over a goal line to score six points for a touchdown and have several additional ways of scoring other amounts of points. Americans wear heavy padding and helmets as part of their uniforms, but Europeans protect themselves only with shin pads. American football games last 60 minutes, but they take longer because of frequent time-outs. European games last 90 minutes, and play rarely stops once the game begins. When Europeans and Americans are playing football, they are not playing the same game.

	European Football	American Football
Ball	1.	2.
Scoring	3.	4.
Players' Padding	5.	6.
Length of Games	7.	8.
Time-outs	9.	10.

Reading Basics · Advanced

Read the two editorials. Then circle the letter of the answer to each question.

Too Young to Drive?

The age at which a teenager can get his or her driver's license ranges from 14 years, 3 months old in the state of South Dakota to as high as 17 years old in the state of New Jersey. If Highway Safety's Adrian Lund gets his way, every teen will have to wait until 17—or even 18. Lund says that car accidents are the leading cause of death among teenagers and wants to increase the driving age. Lund has a point that teenagers do get into accidents. The question is—is it age or how much experience a driver has that is causing the problem? I believe it is a lack of experience because driving is not a skill that is mastered overnight. Instead of raising the age at which teenagers can get a license, why not lower the age at which teenagers can get a learner's permit and drive with parents? That way, teenagers can get more practice, and by the time they are ready to drive on their own, they will have put in many supervised hours behind the wheel. A year won't make much difference, but several years of practice will.

It's Time to Raise the Driving Age

Having to do things you don't like just because they are good for you is all part of being a teenager, and now teens may need to add waiting to drive to the list. It may be unpopular, but, like moms always say, it is for their own good. The Insurance Institute for Highway Safety says that car accidents are the leading cause of death among teenagers. Adrian Lund, the group's leader, says that raising the driving age saves lives, and he may be right. New Jersey is the only state that gives driver's licenses as late as 17, and the number of crash-related deaths in New Jersey is 18 in 100,000. In Connecticut, where teenagers can get learner's permit at 16 and get their license four months later, the death rate is 26 per 100,000. The statistics don't lie, and they tell us that raising the driving age saves lives.

1. One way both editorial writers are alike is that
   A they both think 16 is too young to drive.
   B they both agree that drivers need more practice.
   C they both say that teenagers get into accidents.
   D they both agree that teenagers will like the rule.

2. One way both editorials are different is that
   F only one writer thinks Adrian Lund has a point.
   G only one writer thinks the driving age should be raised.
   H only one writer thinks teenagers are safe drivers.
   J only one writer thinks teenagers will like the rule.

Workplace Skill:
Compare and Contrast a Double Bar Graph

At work, you may need to compare and contrast graphical information. Double bar graphs and double line graphs provide an easy way to quickly compare and contrast two different sets of data. A shop owner may need to compare and contrast sales from different years. The graph below represents the sales for greeting cards at a small shop that sells cards and other items.

Read the graph. Then circle the letter of the answer to each question below the box.

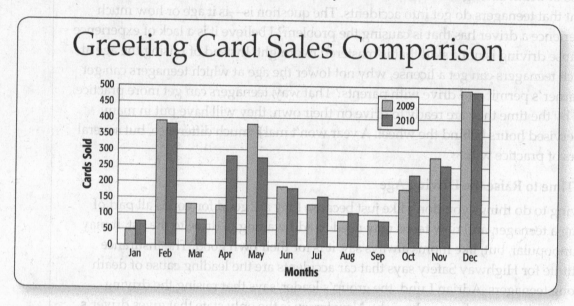

Greeting Card Sales Comparison

1. In what way were 2009 and 2010 alike?

   A   In both years, sales were lowest in January.

   B   In both years, sales were highest in February.

   C   In both years, more cards were sold in May than in April.

   D   In both years, fewer cards were sold in May than in April.

2. In what way were 2009 and 2010 different?

   F   2009 had higher sales in the summer (June, July, August) than 2010 did.

   G   Sales for November and December were higher in 2010.

   H   Sales for April were higher in 2010 than in 2009.

   J   Sales for May were higher in 2010 than in 2009.

3. For both 2009 and 2010, in which month were sales the highest?

   A   February

   B   May

   C   September

   D   December

4. Which statment is true about sales in November in both 2009 and 2010?

   F   Sales were the same.

   G   Sales were higher in 2009.

   H   Sales were higher in 2010.

   J   Sales were at their lowest.

Write for Work

You are the owner of the shop whose sales are described in the graph. Write a short description of card sales for 2009 and 2010. Use words that signal a contrast, such as *unlike*, *however*, and *but*, as well as words that signal comparison, such as *also, in addition*, and *too*. Include a description of which year had the highest sales overall.

  Reading Extension

Turn to "Pirate Chasers: Crime Waves on the High Seas" on page 97 of *Reading Basics Advanced Reader*. After you have read and/or listened to the article, answer the questions below.

Circle the letter of the answer to each question.

1. What is one way in which modern pirates are like famous pirates from the past?

   A   Both force or forced victims to walk the plank.

   B   Both attack or attacked ships to steal their cargo.

   C   Both fly or flew the skull and crossbones.

   D   Both use or used small speedboats.

2. What is one way in which military pirate chasers are different from private pirate chasers?

   F   Private chasers have not had the guerilla warfare training that military chasers have.

   G   Military chasers have not had the counter-terrorism training that private chasers have.

   H   Private chasers do not have the same weaponry as military chasers have.

   J   Military chasers do not have the high-tech boats that private chasers have.

3. What is one way in which the pirates and pirate chasers are alike?

   A   They both track and attack other vessels.

   B   They both have military training.

   C   They both do most of their riskiest work from 1:00 A.M. to 6:00 A.M.

   D   They are both driven by greed.

Write the answer to each question.

4. What is one difference between modern and old-fashioned ships that makes modern ships easier to attack?

_____

_____

5. What is one way modern pirates are different from famous pirates?

_____

_____

Explore Words

ACCENTED AND UNACCENTED SYLLABLES

A syllable is a word part that has one vowel sound. In multisyllabic words, one of the syllables is accented, or stressed. Knowing syllable accent patterns can help you read and spell multisyllabic words.

- In four-syllable words, the accent is usually on the second syllable: re/**frig**/er/ate, a/**dor**/a/ble, un/**us**/u/al.

- In multisyllablic words that end with -ic, the accent is usually on the syllable that comes just before the ending: sym/pa/**thet**/ic, fan/**tast**/ic, e/co/**nom**/ic.

- In multisyllablic words that end with -ity, the accent is usually on the syllable that comes just before the two-syllable ending: e/**qua**/li/ty, per/so/**na**/li/ty, o/**be**/si/ty.

Divide each word into syllables and circle the accented syllable. The first item has been done for you.

1. in/(tel)/li/gent

2. geographic

3. communicate

4. environment

5. necessity

6. mathematics

7. photography

8. characteristic

9. immunity

10. elaborate

11. antiseptic

12. simplicity

PREFIXES

A prefix is a word part that can be added to the beginning of many words. Adding a prefix changes the meaning of the word to which it is added. The prefixes *in-*, *im-*, *ir-*, and *il-* all mean "not." Therefore, *inconvenient* means "not convenient," and *irresponsible* means "not responsible."

Write a word with the prefix *in-*, *im-*, *ir-*, or *il-* that has the meaning of each phrase.

1. not logical _____

2. not appropriate _____

3. not frequently _____

4. not experienced _____

5. not personal _____

6. not competent _____

7. not rational _____

8. not accurate _____

9. not excusable _____

10. not politely _____

Homophones are words that sound the same but have different spellings and different meanings. For example, the words *brews* and *bruise* are homophones.

Choose the word that completes each sentence and write it on the line.

1. Our new puppy _____ on everything! (chews, choose)

2. That story doesn't make any _____. (scents, sense)

3. I think it's _____ that you're going back to school. (great, grate)

4. Have you _____ who won the election? (herd, heard)

5. Australia has a beautiful _____ reef. (coral, choral)

6. The Statue of Liberty is a _____ of freedom. (cymbal, symbol)

7. The son of a king is a _____. (prints, prince)

8. Miguel arranged the chairs in _____. (rows, rose)

9. Aponee caught the _____ and missed a week of work. (flew, flu)

10. Nkeka draws with her _____ hand. (write, right)

ACADEMIC VOCABULARY

Knowing these high-frequency words will help you in many school subjects.

compare	to show how things are alike
contrast	to show how things are different
similar	alike
consider	to think carefully about
frequently	very often

Complete the sentences below using one of the words above.

1. It was difficult to _____ the girls. They had almost nothing in common.

2. Authors are _____ asked about what inspired a particular idea.

3. The writer made sure to _____ the two proposed plans to show how wildly different they were.

4. The sofa Karida bought was _____ to the style of the one she had before.

5. It is best to _____ all of the options carefully before making a decision.

Lesson 3.4

Predict Outcomes

Predicting an outcome means making a logical guess about what will happen next based on the information you have. Predicting keeps you involved in a story or article, and it can add interest to your reading. When you predict, use clues in the text along with your prior knowledge and experience to make guesses that are reasonable, or that make sense, about what will happen next in a passage. Read the example:

A person is packing a suitcase with pajamas, a bathrobe, and a toothbrush.

You might predict that the person is traveling away from home and that he or she will be staying overnight. When predicting outcomes, look for these kinds of clues:

- suggestions of what will happen next in a sequence of events

    Example: *Kirthana grabbed her purse, got in the car, and put on her seatbelt.*

- statements of causes and possible effects

    Example: *Sometimes when it rains, our basement floods.*

- suggestions of how a person has behaved before in a similar situation

    Example: *Oma always cries when she watches sad movies.*

Think about when you've experienced something similar to what you're reading and what the outcome was. Use this information along with text clues to make predictions. Remember to adjust your prediction as you read. New information may be revealed that changes your original prediction. A prediction should make sense with what you have read up to that point, but it may not always turn out to be correct.

Read the passage. Use text clues and what you already know to predict what might happen.

Bargain shoppers should beware of a popular underhanded sales tactic. Valentina noticed the following ad in Thursday's morning newspaper: "32-inch Flat-Panel LCD High-Definition TV—Only $199—Thursday and Friday ONLY!" Valentina got to the store by 10:00 A.M.—just hours after the ad appeared. She was excited and ready to buy, but she discovered that the advertised sets were already sold out. She was about to leave the store when she saw a salesman walking toward her.

Did you predict that the salesman will try to sell Valentina a more expensive TV? The clues are the mention of an underhanded sales tactic and that the advertised TVs were sold out on the morning that the ad appeared. It is likely that only a very small number of the advertised TVs were ever available and that the ad was created to draw people into the store to sell them more expensive merchandise.

Read each passage. Then circle the letter of the answer with the most likely outcome.

Every year between 1949 and 2009, an anonymous admirer visited Edgar Allan Poe's grave and left three roses and a bottle of brandy. The mysterious stranger arrived in the early-morning hours of January 19—Poe's birthday. Several Poe scholars who knew about this annual event once tried to find out who the anonymous admirer was. After midnight on January 19, 1983, they quietly kept watch over Poe's grave.

1. A Around 1:30 A.M., a dark figure in a long coat approached the grave, only to run and flee after seeing the people waiting.

   B They played music and read excerpts from Poe's works.

   C The next day they reported they had seen the ghost of Poe at the grave.

   D Unfortunately, they got frightened and soon went home.

Many people say they don't understand abstract art, but those people are not usually museum curators. In October 1961 the Museum of Modern Art in New York City hung a painting by Henri Matisse, one of the most respected 20th-century French artists. For the next month and a half, more than 100,000 people visited the museum, and most of them viewed the Matisse painting. Art critics also toured the museum on a regular basis, and although none of them reported anything out of the ordinary after viewing Matisse's work, something was very wrong.

2. F The painting was returned to France after a successful showing.

   G The museum's curator admitted that he did not like Matisse's work.

   H A visitor notified embarrassed curators that the painting had been hung upside down.

   J Art critics gave the exhibit a poor review.

When the first light went out at 6:45, the Texas sun had just poked its nose over the horizon, and the hundreds of Navy training planes nestling on the ramp looked like gray ghosts in the dim morning light. Mounting the steps to the squadron control tower, Magi noticed, far off to the north in the dew-infested haze, a scowling bank of black clouds. He felt relieved that he wasn't flying that day. He had, instead, drawn the assignment as tower duty officer.

3. A Magi had to fly through a bad storm.

   B The Navy pilots had to fly through a bad storm.

   C The Navy pilots had an easy day flying, and Magi had a rough day working as tower duty officer.

   D Magi and the Navy pilots took the day off due to the impending storm.

Read each passage and predict the outcome. Then write what you think happened next.

During the first week of September 1900, many people in Galveston Beach, Texas, swam in the great rolling waves that swept in from the Gulf of Mexico. There was a fine surf, yet there was hardly a breath of wind. The barometer was falling, and the wind was picking up—both signs of an impending storm. As a matter of fact, storm warnings had already been sent to people along the Gulf of Mexico. These signs should have aroused some concern in the residents of a town that sat on a sandbar only nine feet above sea level at its highest point, but they didn't.

1. _____

In 1912 a luxury passenger ship had embarked on its very first Atlantic voyage from Southampton, England, to New York City. Early in the night, the captain of the ship had received warnings that icebergs had been spotted in the area where the ship was traveling. The captain changed course, but the enormous liner—with more than 2,200 people on board—sped too quickly through the darkness and toward its destiny.

2. _____

Eric Liddell, a runner from Scotland and a devout Christian, was scheduled to compete in the 100-meter dash in the 1924 Paris Olympics. When Liddell discovered that the qualifying heats were to be held on a Sunday—the Christian Sabbath—he decided to drop out. Liddell was harshly criticized by the Scottish press, who called his decision "unpatriotic." Instead, Liddell trained for the 200-meter and 400-meter races, which did not require him to compromise his religious beliefs.

3. _____

Lashonda worked extra hard on her final paper for her history class. She spent many hours in the library researching her topic and many more hours hunched over a computer writing her paper. When she was done typing, Lashonda read over her five-page paper three times to check for any spelling errors or typos, and she had a friend, who always aced her own papers, read through her paper as well. Lashonda felt confident when she handed it in on the day it was due.

4. _____

Read each passage. Then circle the letter of the most likely ending to the story.

In 1670 British pirate Sir Henry Morgan and his troops were attacking a Spanish fortress in Panama. Inside the fortress were the majority of the Spanish troops in the region. The defenders were strong, and Morgan was thrust back each time he made an assault. According to one story, something happened that altered the outcome of the battle. When one of Morgan's troops took an arrow in the shoulder, he yanked the arrow out, wrapped a burning rag around the end, loaded it into his musket, and fired it back into the fortress.

1. A The soldier died from the arrow wound in his shoulder.

B The arrow proved worthless as it fell at the Spanish general's feet.

C The arrow landed on the enemy's gunpowder, which caused the fortress to explode.

D The arrow killed one unfortunate Spanish soldier.

In April 1865 the Civil War had drawn to a bloody close, and hundreds of Union soldiers were released from the camps where they had been held as prisoners of war. These former prisoners were among the passengers who boarded the steamboat *Sultana* to travel north on the Mississippi River. The vessel's legal capacity was 376 passengers and crew, but that day more than 2,000 men boarded the boat. Early in the morning, the *Sultana's* boilers exploded, causing the ship to erupt in flames.

2. F Most of the men on board were killed.

G Most of the men on board escaped with no injuries.

H The Confederate army came to the men's rescue.

J The men were recaptured and imprisoned by the Confederate army.

Every Saturday morning, Lilia goes to a certain coffee shop and orders a large coffee with cream and two sugars. One Saturday morning, Lilia followed her usual routine—she got up, got dressed, and walked two blocks to the coffee shop—but it was closed due to renovations. Wondering what to do next, Lilia turned and noticed a new coffee shop across the street that she had never tried before.

3. A Lilia went home and made a pot of coffee.

B Lilia went to the new coffee shop and bought a small, black coffee.

C Lilia decided she didn't need any coffee.

D Lilia went to the new coffee shop and bought a large coffee with cream and two sugars.

Workplace Skill:
Predict Outcomes with a Job Posting

Job postings are listings of open jobs at a company or institution. They are usually available online. They describe the position available and the job qualifications. Sonrisa Montgomery is looking for a new position. Her current job requirements are a full-time position, at least $15.00 per hour, no evening work, and availability to work some weekends. She reads the following job posting.

Read the job posting. Then circle the letter of the answer to each question below the box.

Job title	Factory Helper
Hiring pay range	$10.50–$12.27 per hour
Hours per week	32
Other than regular hours (Mon–Fri 8:30–5:00)	Variable schedule may include evenings and weekends. Annually, this position is 41 wks/year. Off periods include 2 months in the summer.
Position summary	The Factory Helper fills bags with bulk items; inserts toy or prize; and packs, labels, or wraps cartons for shipment. Observes highest standards of safety and quality assurance.
Job qualifications	Ability to understand and follow instructions; basic math ability relating to portion control, counting, restocking duties; ability to lift goods or equipment weighing up to 50 pounds; and ability to stand for extended periods of time.
Human Resources contact	Rahman Gleason, Manager, Sweets Candy Factory

1. Based on what Sonrisa's job needs are, what will she most likely do after reading this ad?

   A apply for this position because it is a perfect match with her job needs

   B apply for this position and then ask that the salary level be increased

   C look for another position that more closely matches her job needs

   D apply for this position and state that she will only work days, not evenings

2. Read the sentence. What does the word *variable* mean in this context?
   Variable schedule may include evenings and weekends.

   F sameness

   G consistent

   H predictable

   J changeable

Write for Work

Read the job posting and Sonrisa's job requirements. In your own words, write in a notebook the reasons that this particular job position is or is not a match for Sonrisa.

 ## Reading Extension

Turn to "Ranching: You've Got to Love It" on page 105 of *Reading Basics Advanced Reader*. After you have read and/or listened to the article, answer the questions below.

Circle the letter of the answer to each question.

1. What is one clue in paragraph 1 that helps the reader predict what happens later?

   A The authors describe positive aspects of ranching.

   B The authors ask, "Who wouldn't want to be a rancher?"

   C The authors pose the question, "What are those dark clouds over the ridge?"

   D The authors state, "Have a nice day!"

2. Reread paragraph 4. What do you predict would happen if Gary Skarda used all-terrain vehicles instead of horses?

   F His cattle would probably be fearful and harder to handle.

   G His cattle would probably be easier to handle.

   H He would probably own more cattle.

   J He would probably not make as much money.

3. How do you predict Pat Litton's experience might help her avoid a similar tragedy in the future?

   A She might pay close attention to weather reports to better decide when to carry out some chores.

   B She might decide to stop shearing her sheep.

   C She might move her ranch to an area that does not get much snow.

   D She might sell all of the sheep and cows that she has left.

Write the answer to the question.

4. Do you predict that ranching will continue to be a dangerous profession? Explain your answer.

_____

_____

_____

Explore Words

WORD FAMILIES

A word family is a group of words that have the same base word or root. When you add prefixes, suffixes, and other word endings to a base word or root, the resulting words are members in the same word family. For example, *act, acted, acting, actor, action, react, reaction, active, activate,* and *deactivate* form a word family because they share the base word *act.* The words *tractor, attract, detract, attractive, unattractive, contract,* and *contraction* form a word family because they share the Latin root *tract.*

Create four word families by writing each word in the box under one of the headings below.

| projected | accompany | infrastructure | constructively | unable | companion |
| instructor | disabled | conjecturing | inability | dejectedly | accompanist |

1. ject   **2. company**   **3. struct**   **4. able**

_____   _____   _____   _____

_____   _____   _____   _____

_____   _____   _____   _____

ACCENTED AND UNACCENTED SYLLABLES

A syllable is a word part that has one vowel sound. In multisyllabic words, one of the syllables is accented, or stressed. Knowing syllable accent patterns can help you read and spell multisyllabic words.

- In multisyllablic words that end with *-tion, -sion, -cian,* or *-cial,* the accent is usually on the syllable that comes just before the ending: in/ter/**ven**/tion, fi/**nan**/cial, di/**men**/sion.

- In multisyllablic words that have an *i* that sounds like *y,* the accent is usually on the syllable that comes just before the syllable with the *i*: com/**pan**/ion, con/**ve**/nient.

Divide each word into syllables and circle the accented syllable.

1. familiar   **6.** territorial

2. disciplinarian   **7.** decompression

3. opinion   **8.** bohemian

4. subscription   **9.** intermission

5. ceremonial   **10.** operation

An analogy is a word sentence that describes a relationship between two pairs of words. Here are some common kinds of analogies:

- Synonym: *Kind* : *caring* as *rock* : *stone*. Both pairs are synonyms.
- Antonym: *Less* : *more* as *tall* : *short*. Both pairs are antonyms.
- Grammatical: *Seem* : *seam* as *no* : *know*. Both pairs are homophones.
- Object/Place: *Car* : *garage* as *milk* : *refrigerator*. Both pairs tell where an object is commonly found.
- Object/Use: *Broom* : *sweep* as *phone* : *call*. Both pairs tell how an object is used.
- Part/Whole: *Finger* : *hand* as *toe* : *foot*. The first word in each pair is part of the second word.

Write a word to complete each analogy.

1. *Sun* : *day* as *moon* : _____

2. *Water* : *drink* as *food* : _____

3. *Jam* : *jar* as *cracker* : _____

4. *Complete* : *finish* as *begin* : _____

5. *Scissor* : *cut* as *crayon* : _____

ACADEMIC VOCABULARY

Knowing these high-frequency words will help you in many school subjects.

predict	to make a guess about something that will happen based on clues
outcome	the way something turns out
logical	clearly and soundly reasoned
prior	previous
adjust	to change or alter

Complete the sentences below using one of the words above.

1. I think you'll _____ your opinion after reading this book.

2. My grandfather thinks he was an emperor in a _____ life.

3. Which candidate do you _____ will win the election?

4. You may think her story isn't _____, but I think it makes sense.

5. We're hoping for the best possible _____ of the surgery.

Lesson 3.5

Identify Fact and Opinion

When people write, they often use a mix of facts and opinions. You need to be able to distinguish between the two types of statements to understand what you read. A fact is a statement that can be verified, or proven, in some way. A fact could be a location, a historical event, a statistic, a specific date, or other information that can be tested, looked up in a reference source, or checked in another way. An opinion is a person's belief or viewpoint about something. Some opinions are stated directly and clearly, while other opinions are implied by speech or actions. Words such as *should*, *believe*, *think*, *everyone*, and *no one* often signal opinions. Some forms of writing, such as editorials, memoirs, or personal essays, use a combination of fact and opinion to show the author's viewpoint.

If you want to determine if something is a fact or an opinion, ask yourself if you can prove it by looking in a reference source or testing it. Read the fact and opinion.

> **Fact:** The film *Casablanca* was based on a play titled *Everybody Comes to Rick's*.
>
> **Opinion:** *Casablanca* is the best American film ever made.

Remember that a belief or viewpoint is still an opinion even if many or most people agree with the statement. Another thing to note is that incorrect facts are still facts, because they can be disproved. Read these examples of a fact and a false fact.

> **Fact:** *Casablanca* won the Best Picture Academy Award in 1943.
>
> **False Fact:** *Casablanca* was filmed in Technicolor.

Casablanca was not filmed in Technicolor. You can check this statement by watching the film in black and white or reading a reference on film history, so this is a false fact.

Read the passage. Then circle the statements that are opinions and underline the ones that are facts.

> The Great Wall of China was one of the most impressive engineering projects ever undertaken. The barrier, which was intended to protect central China from invaders, was begun around 403 B.C. It stretches about 5,500 miles from the Bo Gulf of the Yellow Sea to a point far inland. In some areas, the wall has fallen into ruin, but much of it is still standing today. The ruined areas don't detract from the greatness of the whole.

Did you circle "The Great Wall of China was one of the most impressive engineering projects ever undertaken" and "The ruined areas don't detract from the greatness of the whole"? These are opinions in the passage, and the rest are facts that can be proven.

Read each statement. Then write *fact* on the line if the statement is a fact. Write *opinion* on the line if the statement is an opinion.

_____ 1. No one wrote poems that described life in the country better than Robert Frost.

_____ 2. The demand for oil in the United States is growing steadily.

_____ 3. The most beautiful characteristic of Japanese haiku poetry is its delicate brevity.

_____ 4. Changing citizens' attitudes toward conservation is the most important factor in improving our environment.

_____ 5. The blue whale is the largest creature on Earth.

_____ 6. The Louvre in Paris is the most exciting art museum in the world.

_____ 7. The Egyptians hunted and fought with the bow as early as 5000 B.C.

_____ 8. Coffee is a universal beverage that is served in different ways around the world.

_____ 9. In ancient times, people believed that salamanders could put out fires.

_____ 10. Some of the tallest buildings in the world are located in Dubai.

_____ 11. Dubai is an exciting city to visit because of the architecture.

_____ 12. Our country's worst health problem is overeating.

_____ 13. One of the best ways to understand people is to know what makes them laugh.

_____ 14. George Washington was the first president of the United States.

_____ 15. Hawaii is an island located in the Pacific Ocean.

_____ 16. Hawaii is the most romantic spot a couple can choose for a honeymoon.

_____ 17. Pencil lead is actually made from a mineral called graphite.

_____ 18. Pencils are easier to write with than pens.

_____ 19. Pencil drawings are a beautiful form of artwork.

_____ 20. Painting in oil is more difficult than painting in watercolor.

_____ 21. Georgia O'Keeffe is famous in part for her large-scale paintings of flowers.

_____ 22. O'Keeffe lived in New Mexico for several years.

Read the statements. Decide whether each statement is a fact or an opinion. Then write each statement in the appropriate column in the graphic organizer.

Polio is a contagious disease caused by a virus that may attack nerve cells of the brain and spinal cord.

The polio vaccine is one of the most thrilling stories in the history of medicine.

All children should be vaccinated early in life.

In the years following the development of the polio vaccine, the reported cases of polio in the United States were cut by more than 80 percent.

It's amazing that one of the most dreaded of diseases was brought under control by a simple vaccination.

Franklin Delano Roosevelt contracted polio when he was 39 years old.

Despite his disease, he was the greatest president in U.S. history.

Roosevelt hoped that the mineral-rich waters of Warm Springs, Georgia, would cure him.

FDR was a more impressive president than his cousin Teddy Roosevelt.

Fact	Opinion

Read the passage. Then circle the letter of the answer to each question.

In the election of 1928, Herbert Hoover, a Republican, was elected president of the United States over Alfred E. Smith. It was one of the biggest mistakes Americans ever made. He was sworn in as president in March 1929, and just a few months later, in the fall of 1929, the New York Stock Exchange, America's largest stock market, crashed. Many investors lost money, and soon the United States dipped into a depression. It was the worst time in the country's history. During President Hoover's term of office (1929–1933), unemployment rose, national output declined, many factories were idle, and unemployed workers sank into despair. As president, Hoover was a poor leader and an even worse decision maker. Many people could not make their monthly mortgage payments, and families were evicted from their homes by the thousands. Shantytowns, sometimes called Hoovervilles, sprang up all over the country, created from old tin and salvaged wood.

1. What is one fact presented by the passage?

   A It was one of the biggest mistakes Americans ever made.

   B Many investors lost money, and soon the United States dipped into a depression.

   C It was the worst time in the country's history.

   D As president, Hoover was a poor leader and an even worse decision maker.

2. What is one opinion presented by the writer of the passage?

   F As president, Hoover was a poor leader.

   G Many investors lost money.

   H He was sworn in as president in March 1929.

   J Shantytowns, sometimes called Hoovervilles, sprang up all over the country.

3. What is the overall opinion of Herbert Hoover presented by the writer?

   A Hoover was a great president.

   B Americans made the right choice when they elected Hoover.

   C Hoover did the best he could as president.

   D Hoover was not a good leader.

4. If the writer of the passage wanted to add another fact to the passage, which of these could he or she choose?

   F Hoover deserved to have shantytowns named after him.

   G Before his presidency, Hoover had a reputation as a humanitarian.

   H It was terrible that people had to live in homes made of salvaged wood.

   J It would have been better for the country if Alfred E. Smith had won the election.

Workplace Skill: Understand Fact and Opinion in a Letter to School Employees

The following letter is from a new principal to the staff and teachers of the school outlining her goals and endeavors. Remember that an opinion is a person's viewpoint or judgment about an issue, while a fact is something that can be proved.

Read the letter. Then circle the letter of the answer to each question below the box.

Dear Staff,

I'm extremely delighted to have been appointed the new principal at Fairfax Middle School. I wanted to take this opportunity to say how much I look forward to meeting and working with each of you to advance the goals of the teachers and students of Fairfax. Our goal as educators is to provide a sound teaching model based on hands-on learning and critical thinking.

I have been involved in the education field for over 25 years, both as a teacher and as an administrator. I was the principal at Eastside Elementary School for 10 years, where I worked with teachers, students, and parents to expand and deepen the curriculum. I know the challenges teachers face on a daily basis. In today's educational climate, with its stress on passing tests and meeting standards, good teachers are essential. Today's teachers are the best-qualified teachers ever.

I promise to listen to and be open to all your ideas for improving our school and the learning experiences of our students. Our goal should be enriching our students' learning experiences while making your job more enjoyable and challenging. Feel free to seek me out with any ideas or issues you have.

Sincerely,

Alice Phillips

Principal

1. Which statement is an example of a fact from the letter?

   A Teachers are a rare breed.

   B Our goal should be enriching our students' learning experiences.

   C I was the principal at Eastside Elementary School for 10 years.

   D Today's teachers are the best-qualified teachers.

2. Which statement is an opinion?

   F I have been involved in the education field for over 25 years.

   G Today's teachers are the best-qualified teachers ever.

   H I have been both a teacher and an administrator.

   J I have been appointed the new principal at Fairfax Middle School.

Write for Work

You are a teacher at Fairfax Middle School. A friend of yours is thinking of applying for a position as a teacher at your school. She has asked you to tell her about why you like working at Fairfax. In a notebook, write a note or e-mail to your friend stating why you enjoy working at Fairfax. Include both facts and opinions.

 ## Reading Extension

Turn to "Delta Force: Under Cover and Out of Sight" on page 113 of *Reading Basics Advanced Reader*. After you have read and/or listened to the article, answer the questions below.

Circle the letter of the answer to each question.

1. Which of the following statements is a fact?

   A Delta Force members work in the most dangerous settings imaginable.

   B Colonel Charles Beckwith of the U.S. Army was given two years to organize a group of fighters capable of taking on any and all terrorist threats.

   C Delta Force deserves our respect and gratitude.

   D The 18-day selection course is grueling.

2. Which of the following statements is an opinion?

   F United Nations peacekeeping forces had tried to bring humanitarian aid to the city but had failed.

   G Armed only with their sniper rifles and their pistols, the operatives fought off the mob for hours.

   H Delta Force has the best marksmen in the military.

   J Delta Force operatives blend in with the civilian population.

3. Which of the following statements is an opinion?

   A Delta Force operatives change their hairstyle and their clothes to conceal their real identities.

   B Delta Force has its own special fleet of airplanes.

   C Potential candidates for Delta Force are selected by invitation only.

   D Delta Force operatives have more power and less accountability than any U.S. military outfit should have.

Write the answer to the question.

4. What is one fact you learned from this article?

Explore Words

PREFIXES *inter-, super-*

A prefix is a word part that can be added to the beginning of many words. Adding a prefix changes the meaning of a base word or root. For example, the prefix *inter-* means "between or among" or "together," so the word *international* means "among nations," and the word *interlock* means "lock together." The prefix *super-* means "above," "over," or "beyond," so the word *superhuman* means "beyond human."

Choose a word from the box to match the meaning given. Write the word on the line.

superimposed	intervention	supernatural
interstate	interchangeable	superintendent

1. able to be changed among one another _____

2. beyond the known laws of nature _____

3. between or among states _____

4. placed one thing over another _____

5. the act of coming between to change events _____

6. a person in charge of an activity or institution _____

LATIN ROOTS

Many English words have Latin roots. Latin roots have meanings. Knowing the meaning of common Latin roots can help you figure out what an unfamiliar word means. For example, the Latin root *ject* means "throw," and *tract* means "pull."

vid or *vis*	"see"		*aud*	"hear"
liber	"free"		*voc*	"voice"

Circle the Latin root in each word. Then write the letter that shows the word's meaning.

_____ 1. advocate   **a.** to try out for a performing role

_____ 2. invisible   **b.** not able to be seen

_____ 3. audition   **c.** the state of being free from restrictions

_____ 4. liberated   **d.** a person who pleads on someone else's behalf

_____ 5. vocation   **e.** a career to which one is particularly suited

Reading Basics · Advanced

You can usually figure out the meaning of unfamiliar words by using context clues. Context is other words, phrases, and sentences that surround the unfamiliar word.

Read the passage. Use the context to help you figure out the meaning of each underlined word. Then match each word in the first column with its definition in the second column. Write the matching letter on the line.

> During the Italian Renaissance, people with <u>expertise</u> in many fields were respected. The <u>renowned</u> painter Leonardo da Vinci was one such Renaissance man. He studied constantly and was seen as an accomplished painter, sculptor, engineer, and scientist. Da Vinci worked hard to develop his <u>sundry</u> talents. He applied himself <u>diligently</u> to every project. He succeeded more often than not.

_____ **1.** expertise   **a.** famous

_____ **2.** renowned   **b.** various

_____ **3.** sundry   **c.** with great care

_____ **4.** diligently   **d.** skill or knowledge in a particular field

Knowing these high-frequency words will help you in many school subjects.

fact   a piece of information that can be shown to be true or false

opinion   someone's thoughts or beliefs about something

prove   to show the existence, truth, or validity of

viewpoint   a particular attitude or way of thinking about something

decline   to become smaller or to decrease

Complete the sentences below using one of the words above.

1. There was no way to _____ whether the man had cheated or not.

2. It is a _____ that Springfield is the capital of Illinois.

3. The facts and opinions in the editorial in the paper really show the writer's _____.

4. It is Zhang's _____ that red is a better color for the walls than purple, and I can see her viewpoint.

5. After a third of the workers were laid off, production began to _____.

Lesson 3.6

Identify Genre

The term genre refers to a category or type of art, music, film, or literature. The three major literary genres are prose, poetry, and drama. Within each of these genres are a number of subgenres, which are divisions into which each main genre is split.

Prose is writing that is similar to everyday speech and language, and it includes fiction and nonfiction.

- Fiction is imaginary writing, although the characters may seem real or even be based on real people. Fiction is commonly written in the form of a novel, a novella, or a short story. Some varieties of fiction include science fiction, historical fiction, romance, mystery, and folktales.

- Nonfiction deals with real people, places, and events. Biographies (stories of a person's life), autobiographies (stories of one's own life), memoirs, newspaper and magazine articles, reports, diary entries, letters, and essays are all forms of nonfiction.

Poetry differs from prose by emphasizing the line rather than the sentence. Poets paint pictures of images or ideas, using carefully chosen words and sounds. A poem may or may not rhyme, may be long or short, and may create one or more images.

Drama is typically written in the form of a script, and it is intended to be viewed by an audience. When drama is presented, actors generally speak and perform as the characters, although drama can also be animated or even silent. Drama can be a skit, play, movie, or television show.

Read the passage. Then decide to what genre or subgenre it belongs.

As soon as her hostess left the room, Miss Picket put down her teacup and examined the marks on the gleaming varnish of the table. The marks were shallow, but she could just about make them out. Glancing quickly at the door, she pulled out her pocket magnifying glass and leaned in. Just as she'd thought, the indentations had been made by someone writing forcefully on a sheet of paper with a ballpoint pen. She quickly copied the text of the phantom letter into her notebook, underlining the name George Weathersby. She now had one more person to add to her list of suspects.

This passage is a subgenre of fiction known as mystery, and it tells the story of an imaginary woman named Miss Picket. She keeps a list of suspects, leading the reader to assume that a crime has occurred and that Miss Picket is attempting to discover who committed it.

Read each passage. Then identify its genre or subgenre by writing *poetry*, *fiction*, *nonfiction*, or *drama*.

Giuseppe Garibaldi was the hero of the Italian Risorgimento, the 19th-century movement to unify Italy. His success was based on military success and on his successful use of propaganda to persuade supporters to the cause of unification. He was one of the great masters of guerrilla warfare, leading the majority of the military victories of the movement. Garibaldi was so celebrated internationally that President Lincoln offered Garibaldi a command in the Union army during the Civil War.

1. _____

Religious freedom has been a political issue around the world for many centuries. The Edict of Nantes, a decree issued in 1598 by the Catholic King Henry IV of France, was a milestone in the development of religious freedom. The edict was the first official document evidencing religious toleration in a large European country. It granted religious freedom to Henry's Protestant subjects, the Huguenots, ending 50 years of domestic fighting and religious separation.

2. _____

Winona: We'll be late if you don't hurry. (*Checks watch.*)

(*Hatima remains seated and types into a computer.*)

Hatima: (*slowly, distracted*) Yeah. Coming.

Winona: You don't even have your shoes on.

(*Hatima stops typing but does not stand up.*)

Hatima: What? They're right here.

Winona: Never mind. We've missed the 2:30 bus. We might as well stay home now.

3. _____

There once was a girl from White Bluff,
who stormed out of the house in a huff.
She kicked a big rock
and got dirt on her sock,
that mad, wounded girl from White Bluff.

4. _____

Read each passage. Then identify the category of writing using the list in the box.

romance	autobiography	science fiction
historical fiction	mystery	folktale

Sitting on the fire escape, Sanj caught the first glimpse of morning light rise over the tall buildings of the city. As he scanned the world from his metal perch, Sanj thought he heard muffled screaming. Before he could determine what it was, a woman with long black hair threw open a window across the alley, locked eyes with Sanj, and mouthed the word, "help." Sanj was stunned and a little confused. He thought he should call 911. As Sanj was pondering his next move, the woman calmly closed the window and drew the curtains, as if nothing had happened.

1. _____

Walking through the park on her way to work, Mariama had often noticed—or rather heard—a man, with a soulful voice, playing the guitar. She never paid much attention to him. On one cold Friday morning, Mariama tripped and fell right in front of the man. As he helped her up, Mariama noticed that he had beautiful dark eyes, curly dark hair, and a charming smile, and she was instantly smitten.

2. _____

Growing up, I lived in a small farmhouse on a dairy farm. Each morning before school, I would go out and complete my chores, which included collecting eggs from our chickens and milking our cow. On dark, cold days, I would often dream of a life in the big city, a life without chores around every corner. Determined to leave, I saved every penny I had and at the age of 19, I boarded a bus for New York City.

3. _____

As the war got closer to home, Susannah kept thinking she could smell gunpowder in the air. Samuel thought that her fears and anxieties were irrational, but he didn't hear the whispers in the post office and at the general store. Susannah was not the only nervous one—the whole town was holding their breath in wait of the day General Grant and his northern men would show up at their front doors.

4. _____

Read each passage. Then circle the letter of the category of writing to which the passage belongs.

After Anjel screwed the last panel back in place, she held her breath and waited, but nothing happened. She stared, clutching her screwdriver, but the lights were distinctly dim and the speakers were deafeningly silent. Blinking back tears from her eyes, Anjel considered each of the steps she had just completed. She'd connected every wire and rebooted each system exactly as the schematic indicated. Just as she was coming to the conclusion that her original design was fundamentally flawed, she heard a small whirring sound. The check lights on the android's fingertips began lighting from yellow to green, and the eyes opened suddenly. Anjel dropped her screwdriver, ignoring the clatter of metal on tile, and waited for her android to speak.

1. **A** drama   **C** science fiction
   B poetry   **D** memoir

Even as a young child, I was a science fanatic. My education was scientific, and I even went so far as to write a short article for a scientific magazine when I was just 11 years old. Science, to my way of thinking, was, and is even now, the only reliable means we possess to discover the truth about our world and about ourselves.

2. **F** autobiography   **H** romance
   G drama   **J** poetry

Binta: *(looking anxiously at Omar)* Where are you going?

(Omar holds his jacket in one hand and his keys in another.)

Omar: Out.

(Binta plays with the wedding ring on her finger.)

Binta: When will you be home?

Omar: Later.

Binta: *(quietly)* Will you call when you know more?

Omar: Yeah, sure.

(Omar walks out the door.)

(Binta looks over to see Omar's cell phone still sitting on the kitchen table.)

3. **A** myth   **C** diary entry
   B poetry   **D** drama

Workplace Skill:
Identify Genre in Business Documents

Most workplace writing is nonfiction. You select a particular form of business writing depending on the purpose of the communication and the audience you want to reach. Employers need to know that employees can read, understand, and use the information communicated in these different kinds of materials. As an employee, you need to identify and find information and understand how to apply instructions to various situations.

Read the passage. Then circle the letter of the answer to each question below the box.

Categories and Examples of Business Writing

Business Forms
* Job Application Forms
* Expense Forms

Consumer Materials
* Want Ads
* Job Descriptions

Graphics
* Graphs and Charts
* Diagrams

Employee Handbook
* Attendance Policies
* Holiday and Time-off Policies

Employee Internal Communication
* E-mails
* Letters

Training Manuals
* Project Start-up Procedures
* Technical Writers' Training Materials

Procedural Documents
* Recycling Procedures
* Customer Return Instructions

---

1. If you need to submit a report that visually shows information on unemployment statistics, which form of business writing would you use?

 A a graph or chart

 B an expense form

 C an e-mail

 D a job description

2. If you need to communicate informally with a coworker about an upcoming meeting, which form of business writing would be best?

 F a training manual

 G a procedural document

 H an employee handbook

 J an internal e-mail

Write the answer to the question.

3. In what situation might you write project start-up procedures?

_____

_____

Write for Work

On your list of things remaining to be done this week at work are the following items:

    Item 1: communicate to a coworker that you will be late for a business lunch

    Item 2: write a formal reply to a client who has requested company information

    Item 3: draft a recycling policy for your department

For each item, identify the form of business writing that would be best. Select one of the items to complete and write a draft in a notebook.

Workplace Extension

Overtime or Not?

Mark Verga and Luis Raphael work as night stockers in a large home decor store. Their responsibilities are to maintain adequate product inventory levels, stock shelves, refill displays, and keep their department area clean and well organized. They also need to load, unload, and move heavy, bulky products within the store and warehouse. The heaviest shopping period is fast approaching, and management has asked all employees to work extra hours to accommodate market demands at this busy time. Luis is able to reschedule his plans to go to the movies so that he can work overtime. Mark has family and educational commitments at this time that he cannot change and that prevent him from working extra hours.

Circle the letter of the answer to each question.

1. Luis's response shows that he is
   - **A** mindful of safety on the job.
   - **B** flexible.
   - **C** irresponsible.
   - **D** proud and haughty at work.

2. What should Mark do?
   - **F** tell his manager that under no circumstances will he be able to work extra hours
   - **G** explain his commitments to his manager
   - **H** do nothing and hope his absence is not noticed
   - **J** tell Luis that he should not have offered to work extra because it makes him look bad

Write the answer to the question.

3. You have been asked to work extra hours, but your commitments do not allow you to do this. Write a note to

your manager explaining your situation. _____

_____

Explore Words

ANALOGIES

An analogy is a word sentence that describes a relationship between two pairs of words. To complete an analogy, you need to figure out the relationship between the two words. Read this part/whole analogy: *Wings : plane* as *wheels : car*. In the example, the first word in each pair represents part of the second word; wings are part of a plane and wheels are part of a car. There are several other common types of analogies: synonym, antonym, grammatical, object/place, and object/use.

Write a word to complete each analogy.

1. *Chicken : egg* as *cow :* _____

2. *Rake : leaves* as *broom :* _____

3. *Glasses : eyes* as *hearing aids :* _____

4. *More : most* as *less :* _____

5. *Airplane : flying* as *ship :* _____

6. *Belief : disbelief* as *trust :* _____

7. *Woman : women* as *tooth :* _____

8. *Generous : stingy* as *artificial :* _____

MULTIPLE SUFFIXES

A suffix is a word part that can be added to the end of many words. Adding a suffix changes the meaning of a base word or root. Some words have more than one suffix, and the meaning of each one affects the meaning of the whole word. For example, the suffixes *-less* and *-ness* can be added to the base word *sleep* to form the word *sleeplessness*, meaning "the state of being without sleep." Some other common suffixes include *-al, -ly, -tion,* and *-ful*.

Circle the word in each sentence that has more than one suffix. Then draw a slash (/) between the suffixes.

1. My daughter's class is going on an educational field trip to the art museum.

2. The soprano sang her solo just beautifully.

3. I appreciated everyone's helpfulness during my recent illness.

4. He fearlessly helped people to safety outside the burning building.

5. Modern appliances allow us to do many jobs effortlessly.

SPELLING: HOMOPHONES

Homophones are words that sound alike but are spelled differently and have different meanings. For example, *weather* and *whether* are homophones.

Complete each sentence using a homophone from the box.

paced	paste	peace	piece	quartz	quarts
waist	waste	forth	fourth	rung	wrung
straight	strait	sight	cite		

1. Do you think that _____ in the Middle East is possible?

2. We shut off the faucet so we won't _____ water.

3. I _____ the floor with worry until he got home.

4. Please pick up two _____ of milk on your way here.

5. This is the _____ time I've had to work overtime this week.

6. The bottom _____ of the ladder is broken, so be careful.

7. Be sure to _____ your sources in your article.

8. Drive _____ down MLK Boulevard until you get to the light.

ACADEMIC VOCABULARY

Knowing these high-frequency words will help you in many school subjects.

genre a type of art, music, film, or literature

drama a story meant to be performed by actors before an audience

prose written or spoken language in ordinary form

audience the people who watch or listen to something

list a set of items considered to be in the same category

Complete the sentences below using one of the words above.

1. The _____ applauded loudly at the end of each act.

2. The author was well known in his particular _____.

3. You can find that play in the _____ section of the bookstore.

4. The author disliked poetry, so she always wrote in _____.

5. Balkar made a _____ of all the things he needed from the store.

Unit 3 Review

Make Generalizations

Generalizations present conclusions that apply to many people, facts, events, or situations. They can sum up what has been said or introduce more specific information that will follow. When you make a generalization, you come to a broad conclusion based on specific pieces of evidence.

Recognize Author's Effect and Intention

An author's intention is what he or she hopes the reader will take away after reading his or her text. Style techniques such as word choice, sentence structure, imagery, and figurative language create effects, such as humor, sarcasm, excitement, anger, or suspense.

Compare and Contrast

A writer who wants to describe two or more people or things might compare them by describing the ways in which they are alike. He or she might contrast them by describing the ways in which they differ.

Predict Outcomes

Predicting an outcome means making a logical guess about what will happen next based on the information you have. When you predict, use clues in the text along with your prior knowledge and experience to make guesses that are reasonable about what will happen next in a passage.

Identify Fact and Opinion

It is important for readers to distinguish between fact and opinion. A fact is a statement that can be verified, or proved, in some way. An opinion is a personal belief or viewpoint; it's a statement that cannot be proved.

Identify Genre

There are three main literary genres: poetry, prose, and drama. Prose is divided into fiction and nonfiction. Fiction is imaginary writing, while nonfiction deals with real people, places, and events. Each of these can be further divided into additional categories. Poetry focuses on creating a picture with words. Drama is meant to be performed for an audience.

Unit 3 Assessment

Read each passage. Then circle the letter of the answer to each question.

It was a chilly day in what had been an unseasonably warm winter. Abba hesitated, but Jorga hurried to lace up her skates that day.

Abba gazed out at the frozen pond. "I don't think it's thick enough to skate on," she muttered. "Remember when those kids fell through the ice last winter?"

"Relax, Abba," scoffed Jorga. "You always think of something to worry about. Just try to have a good time for once."

"I know, but there have been too many accidents on this pond. Hey, wait!" Abba called frantically as she watched Jorga skate off blithely out to the middle of the pond.

---

1. What do you predict will happen next?

   A Abba will decide to go home.

   B Jorga will decide not to skate.

   C Abba will have a good time skating.

   D Jorga will fall through the ice.

2. What kind of effect does the author create?

   F angry

   G exciting

   H humorous

   J ominous

3. Which sentence gives the reader a hint about the outcome?

   A "Remember when those kids fell through the ice last winter?"

   B Abba gazed out at the frozen pond.

   C "You always think of something to worry about."

   D "Just try to have a good time for once."

Tennis was first introduced to the United States in 1874 by Mary Ewing Outerbridge, who brought rackets and balls from Bermuda. However, it's possible that a man in Nahant, Massachusetts, may have actually had a tennis set first. The first tennis court was laid out on grass at the Staten Island Cricket and Baseball Club, of which Mary Ewing Outerbridge's brother was director. Within seven years, the sport had become so popular that the U.S. National Lawn Tennis Association, now known as the U.S. Tennis Association, was formed, and competitions were held.

---

4. What is the writer's intention for writing?

   F to convince people to take up tennis as a hobby

   G to compare tennis to cricket

   H to describe the origins of tennis in the United States

   J to describe how tennis was invented

5. To what genre or subgenre does this passage belong?

   A nonfiction

   B romance

   C drama

   D science fiction

The members of the U.S. Supreme Court look carefully at each case. In 1969 in the case of *Tinker v. Des Moines Independent Community School District*, the justices voted in favor of students who wore black armbands to school to protest the Vietnam War. The students felt this was part of their First Amendment right to free speech and that they did not pose a threat to the school or students. Most justices agreed.

In contrast, the 1988 case *Hazelwood School District v. Kuhlmeier* resulted in a different decision, though the setting was the same. The justices did not uphold what some high school students believed to be free speech. The principal had censored several pages of the school newspaper, and the court upheld his right to do so, stating that any publication that seemed to be approved of by the school had to be consistent with the school's educational mission.

6. What is one way in which the cases are alike?

  F The Supreme Court ruled in favor of the students in each case.

  G The Supreme Court ruled in favor of the schools in each case.

  H Both cases involved decisions on freedom of speech.

  J Both cases involved decisions on peaceful protest.

7. What two items are being compared and contrasted in this passage?

  A two school policies

  B two Supreme Court decisions

  C newspapers and war protests

  D different parts of the Bill of Rights

A stock market provides a way for investors to buy or sell stocks of a corporation. Ranked by the number of stocks bought and sold, the Nasdaq Stock Market is the largest stock market in the world. The Nasdaq Stock Market is made up of a complex network of investors and investment companies linked by computers. The New York Stock Exchange (NYSE) is the second-largest stock market. The trading of stocks on the trading floor of the NYSE is old-fashioned, so it should close its doors. Companies currently listed on the NYSE should switch to the more modern Nasdaq Stock Market. In addition, we should also extend federal insurance protection to investors to guarantee that investors don't lose money on their stocks.

8. To what genre or subgenre does this passage belong?

  F biography

  G poetry

  H editorial

  J drama

9. Which of the following is an opinion?

  A The Nasdaq Stock Market is the largest stock market in the world.

  B A stock market provides a way for investors to buy or sell stocks of a corporation.

  C The New York Stock Exchange (NYSE) is the second-largest stock market.

  D Companies currently listed on the NYSE should switch to the more modern Nasdaq Stock Market.

The human body has many parts. Some body parts—such as the spleen—have vital functions but are not necessary to staying alive. The major body organs, such as the heart, liver, and lungs, are important and necessary. Without a heart or liver, for example, no one can live. Many people choose to become organ donors. They help others by agreeing to donate their healthy organs when they die. Organ donors are the most compassionate people in the world. Many states have a provision on a driver's license to indicate that the driver has chosen to become an organ donor. After death, their organs may be transplanted into the bodies of people who need them.

10. Which of the following statements is an opinion?

    F The human body has many parts.

    G Some body parts have vital functions but are not necessary to staying alive.

    H Many people choose to become organ donors.

    J Organ donors are the most compassionate people in the world.

11. From this passage you can generalize that

    A many organ donations help save lives.

    B organ donors think everyone should donate.

    C all organ donors have driver's licenses.

    D the heart is an important organ.

The Arctic tundra is sometimes thought of as a cold desert, but there is more life there than you might think. The Arctic landscape is beautiful. During summer the tundra is covered in lichens and small plants, such as mosses and grasses. Additionally, you may find some wolves, foxes, and lemmings as well as caribous and reindeer, traveling in herds. Many birds, such as the snow bunting, white-fronted goose, and merlin, migrate to the tundra for the summer. Bacteria and fungi live in the soil, and a few Arctic foxes and musk oxen live in the tundra throughout the year.

12. What generalization can you make from this passage?

    F The climate of the tundra cannot support living things.

    G Despite its cold climate, the tundra supports many kinds of life at certain times of the year.

    H No animals can survive in a freezing desert.

    J Many animals live in the tundra all year.

13. Which of the following is an opinion about the Arctic?

    A The Arctic landscape is beautiful.

    B During summer the tundra is covered in lichens and small plants, such as mosses and grasses.

    C Bacteria and fungi live in the soil.

    D Arctic foxes and musk oxen live in the tundra throughout the year.

Read the procedural document. Then circle the letter of the answer to each question.

Processing a Send Sale

A send sale is a sale that is processed in our store registers and shipped to a client. It is an easy way to make a sale. Phone orders occur when customers call our store looking for a specific item, and online orders come through the company e-mail system. If you receive a phone order, place the customer on hold while you search for the item in the store or in the stock room. Confirm with the customer that it is the correct item by describing the color, fabric, cut, etc. Fill out a yellow send-sale slip with the customer's billing address, shipping address, credit card information, and phone number. Ring the sale into the register, place the item in a box, and fill out a mailing slip. Place the yellow slip in the send-sale folder and place the box in the designated pickup location.

The process for an online order is very similar to the process for a phone order, but the information will come via e-mail. Search the sales floor and stock room for the item and verify the item number. The e-mail will have all of the customer's payment information. Print the e-mail, ring the sale into the register, and place the printout in the send-sale folder. Fill out a mailing slip and leave the box in the pickup location.

14. What is one way in which phone orders and online orders are similar?

   F   Both require the salesperson to verify the item number.

   G   In both cases, someone will call with an item request.

   H   Both require the salesperson to fill out a yellow card.

   J   Both require the salesperson to fill out a mailing slip.

15. What is one way in which phone orders and online orders are different?

   A   In a phone order, the salesperson should search the stock room, but in an online order, the salesperson should only look on the sales floor.

   B   In a phone order, a customer calls looking for an item, but in an online order, the request comes via e-mail.

   C   In a phone order, the salesperson must ring the sale into the register, but in an online order, the sale has already been processed.

   D   In a phone order, a record should be placed in the send-sale folder, but in an online order, no paper record is kept.

16. Which of the following is an opinion?

   F   It is an easy way to make a sale.

   G   The process for an online order is very similar to the process for a phone order.

   H   Confirm with the customer that it is the correct item by describing the color, fabric, cut, etc.

   J   The e-mail will have all of the customer's payment information.

Read the bulletin board notice. Then circle the letter of the answer to each question.

Company Break Policy, Debbie's Dress Shop

All employees working a six-hour shift or more are entitled to a one-hour lunch break and must take a break of at least one-half hour. It is very important that all employees correctly sign in and out when leaving for their break so that the company records will be accurate in case of an audit.

When employees report for work each day, they should check with a manager to find out when their break is scheduled. Breaks are staggered throughout the day to ensure that no more than two people are on break at any given time. This is done to ensure proper coverage of the sales floor. If employees wish to change the time of their break, they should consult with the manager on duty to see if such a change is possible. If employees find themselves unable to stop work at their break time because they are engaged with a customer, they should alert their manager as soon as possible. It is not permissible to skip a meal break in order to end the workday early because there would be no record of your time-earned break, which the company would need in case of an audit by the Department of Labor.

17. What generalization can be made from the second paragraph?

   A   It is important for employees to communicate with managers.

   B   All break times are set, and no changes are allowed.

   C   Breaks are more important than helping customers.

   D   It is fine to come in late or leave early if you skip your break.

18. Based on the notice, what outcome can you predict if employees are not allowed to take breaks?

   F   Productivity will go up.

   G   The company may receive a warning or a fine.

   H   The company will falsify records of employee breaks.

   J   Customers will stop doing business with the company.

19. What do you think the writer's intention was for creating this bulletin board notice?

   A   to scare employees into working through their breaks

   B   to explain the importance of proper sales floor coverage

   C   to explain the importance of properly taking and documenting breaks

   D   to encourage employees to learn about their state's laws regulating work hours

20. If an employee is scheduled to take a meal break between 1:00 and 2:00 P.M. and she finds herself leaving for her break 35 minutes late, what might happen to the person scheduled to take a break between 2:00 and 3:00 P.M.?

   F   The second person will leave on time, and there won't be proper coverage on the floor.

   G   The second person will have to wait and take his or her break late.

   H   The first person will not get to take a meal break.

   J   The second person will not be allowed to take a meal break.

Circle the letter of the answer to each question.

21. Which word means the opposite of the underlined word?

sensible person

- **A** foolish
- **B** reasonable
- **C** sensitive
- **D** logical

22. Which word means "the state of being an owner"?

- **F** ownerness
- **G** ownness
- **H** ownership
- **J** ownship

23. Which word does NOT belong in the word family?

- **A** credit
- **B** incredible
- **C** create
- **D** credibility

24. Which answer shows *cantankerous* divided correctly into syllables? The accented syllable is boldfaced.

- **F** cant/an/ke/ro/us
- **G** can/tan/**ker**/ous
- **H** cant/ank/e/rous
- **J** can/tan/ker/ous

25. Which word correctly completes the sentence?

Kim and Roberto forgot where they parked _____ car.

- **A** they're
- **B** their
- **C** there
- **D** theyr

26. Which word means "having the characteristics of industry"?

- **F** industrial
- **G** industrious
- **H** industries
- **J** subindustry

27. Which word has the same or almost the same meaning as the underlined word?

Georgia was extremely peevish. She snapped at her friends and didn't have a kind word for anyone.

- **A** youthful
- **B** friendly
- **C** ill-natured
- **D** adventurous

28. Which analogy is correct?

- **F** *thermometer : temperature* as *garage : car*
- **G** *thermometer : temperature* as *ruler : yardstick*
- **H** *thermometer : temperature* as *scale : weight*
- **J** *thermometer : temperature* as *soap : dirt*

29. Which word means "having the characteristics of influence"?

- **A** influenting
- **B** uninfluenced
- **C** superinfluence
- **D** influential

30. Which word means "not mobile"?

- **F** inmobile
- **G** immobile
- **H** irmobile
- **J** ilmobile

31. Which word has more than one suffix?

- **A** fixable
- **B** carelessness
- **C** doubtful
- **D** celebration

32. Which word means "among faiths"?

- **F** faithful
- **G** superfaith
- **H** interfaith
- **J** multifaith

Posttest

Read each passage. Then circle the letter of the answer to each question.

Though no one knows exactly how ancient people discovered fire, they probably saw it in its natural form long before they learned how to make it themselves. Lightning causes forest fires, which were just as common in the ancient past as they are today. Fires were also produced from the hot lava of volcanoes and from collisions of stones. What people saw taught them how to use fire. Modern historians think that before ancient people knew how to make fire, they carried it with them from place to place in order to keep it burning.

1. What are some natural causes of fire?

   A   lava and lightning

   B   lava and rivers

   C   tides and rocks

   D   sand and lightning

2. What conclusion can you draw about why early people carried fire with them from place to place?

   F   They relied on fire in their daily lives.

   G   They used fire to light the way as they traveled.

   H   They traded fire for food and clothing.

   J   They used fire to announce their arrival.

(1) For thousands of years, thieves have ingeniously outsmarted the protective devices created by ancient Egyptian tomb makers. (2) Bandits have found their way through impossible mazes, detected decoys, and avoided carefully laid traps. (3) Archaeologist Sir Flinders Petrie believed that the robbers of one tomb found their way through the opening of a labyrinth with the help of a master plan that an informer had given to them. (4) The thieves who looted the great burial mound at Deir el Bahri did so before archaeologists discovered the site. (5) Scientists started cataloging the site's treasures only after valuable stolen artifacts from the tomb were discovered on the black market.

3. Which sentence states the main idea of this passage?

   A   sentence 1

   B   sentence 3

   C   sentence 4

   D   sentence 5

4. After the looting of Deir el Bahri, what artifacts did scientists see on the black market?

   F   gold jewelry

   G   wooden sculptures

   H   funeral masks

   J   not stated

5. What is the best paraphrase of sentence 1?

   A   Tombs have protective devices.

   B   The creators of ancient Egyptian tombs placed devices to guard the tombs, but thieves have outsmarted these devices for thousands of years.

   C   Robbers were smarter than the people who set traps in tombs. The traps were not that good.

   D   Egyptian tombs are much easier to rob than people think.

Tobacco, unlike alcohol, has never been prohibited in the United States, but in both colonial and modern times there have been some strict laws regarding tobacco usage. The first smoking law in New England was passed in the 1600s and was intended to reduce the risk of fires caused by smoking. Later, other colonies passed laws to limit or prevent smoking. In 1964 the United States government passed a law requiring all packaging and advertising for cigarettes to carry a health warning. Beginning in the 1990s, many states adopted laws that restricted smoking in public places. In 1996 the federal government finalized regulations to prevent people under the age of 18 from smoking. People are divided on the appropriateness and fairness of smoking legislation. Proponents of antismoking laws uphold the rights of nonsmokers. Smokers are selfish if they think that their right to smoke is more important than the health of the people around them.

6. Which sentence expresses an opinion about tobacco-use laws?

F In 1964 the United States government passed a law requiring all packaging and advertising for cigarettes to carry a health warning.

G Beginning in the 1990s, many states adopted laws that restricted smoking in public places.

H People are divided on the appropriateness and fairness of smoking legislation.

J Smokers are selfish if they think that their right to smoke is more important than the health of the people around them.

7. The author's purpose in this paragraph is to

A tell readers about some U.S. smoking laws.

B convince readers that smoking is dangerous.

C persuade readers to campaign for stricter smoking laws.

D inform readers about the effects of secondhand smoke.

8. If you wanted to look up information about which state produced the most tobacco last year, which reference source might you use?

F almanac

G atlas

H thesaurus

J road atlas

9. When was the first smoking law passed?

A 1600s

B 1964

C 1990s

D 1996

(1) Frank Lloyd Wright was one of the most creative influences in modern American architecture. (2) He designed buildings that blended with and enhanced the natural environment. (3) In the Midwest, where he lived most of his life, he created houses that were low and broad like the prairies they occupied. (4) Wright was a pioneer of open interior spaces, which he preferred to traditional, box-like rooms. (5) He also designed urban skyscrapers and other large-scale buildings, such as the futuristic Unity Temple in Oak Park, Illinois, and the Guggenheim Museum in New York City. (6) Frank Lloyd Wright provided a novel way of looking at forms, spaces, and materials that helped to guide American architecture in a new direction.

10. What is the meaning of the word *novel* as used sentence 6?

    F innovative

    G a book of fiction

    H made-up

    J strange

11. What style technique is used in sentence 3?

    A action

    B personification

    C simile

    D metaphor

12. How did Frank Lloyd Wright use building materials to emphasize his prairie style?

    F He used wood and other materials as they appeared in nature.

    G He used paint that blended in with the colors of the prairie.

    H He used concrete to make the buildings stand out in the natural environment.

    J not stated

13. You can infer that the author's intention is to show that

    A all modern architecture is based on the ideas of Frank Lloyd Wright.

    B Frank Lloyd Wright was a highly overrated architect.

    C American architecture should have followed more traditional styles.

    D Frank Lloyd Wright contributed much to American architecture.

14. What is the genre or subgenre of this passage?

    F biography

    G romance

    H poetry

    J diary entry

Cardiopulmonary resuscitation (CPR) is a lifesaving procedure used to maintain respiration and blood circulation in a person whose heartbeat and breathing have stopped. It is most commonly administered when the victim has had a severe heart attack or serious accident. First the rescuer checks to see if the victim is unconscious. If there is no response from the victim, the rescuer calls for help before administering CPR. The victim is placed on his or her back, and the rescuer checks for a pulse by feeling one of the large arteries in the victim's neck. If a pulse cannot be detected, the rescuer begins chest compressions by placing both hands—one on top of the other—on the lower part of the victim's breastbone and compressing the chest 30 times. Then the rescuer presses down on the victim's forehead and lifts the bony part of the chin to clear the victim's air passages. The rescuer pinches the victim's nostrils shut, takes a deep breath, and blows into the victim's mouth to inflate the lungs. The rescuer gives two slow breaths and releases the victim's nostrils to allow him or her to exhale. This is followed by 30 more chest compressions. This procedure should be performed continuously until the victim's heartbeat and breathing resume. When help arrives, the victim must be taken to the hospital for further care.

15. CPR is most commonly administered

   A when the victim is choking.

   B when the victim has had a severe heart attack or serious accident.

   C when the victim has been burned.

   D when the victim has high blood pressure.

16. What is the first thing a rescuer does to the victim?

   F pinch the victim's nostrils

   G establish an open air passage

   H determine if he or she is unconscious

   J compress the chest 30 times

17. What pattern does the rescuer follow when administering CPR?

   A 1 breath, 30 compressions, 1 breath

   B 2 compressions, 30 breaths, 2 compressions

   C 1 breath, 30 compressions, 2 breaths

   D 30 compressions, 2 breaths, 30 compressions

18. As used in the paragraph, *administer* means

   F "dispense or apply a remedy."

   G "manage the running of a business."

   H "a religious leader."

   J "promote sales by making something known."

19. What should a rescuer do before starting CPR on an unresponsive victim?

   A wash his or her hands

   B maintain the victim's respiration

   C call for help

   D take the victim to the hospital

20. You can conclude that when help is needed a rescuer should call

   F 911 for an EMT or ambulance.

   G a friend who knows CPR.

   H a relative of the victim.

   J the victim's doctor.

Read the smartphone comparison chart. Then circle the letter of the answer to each question.

Touchsmart Phone

$229.99*

built-in GPS

2.4" × 0.5" × 4.6"

requires data plan

full touch screen

talk time up to 575 minutes

6 megapixel camera

HD camcorder

Grapeseed Phone

$159.99*

GPS add-on optional

2.8" × 0.55" × 4.8"

requires data plan

full touch screen

talk time up to 340 minutes

8 megapixel camera

* After mail-in rebate. New two-year activation required.

21. What does the asterisk after the price listed mean?

  A Nothing. It is decorative.

  B It tells you that the price could change at any time.

  C It tells you that there is more information that affects the price somewhere on the page.

  D It tells you that this price is only good in the continental United States.

22. If you do not sign up for a new two-year contract, how much will the Grapeseed phone cost?

  F $159.99

  G $229.99

  H $259.99

  J not stated

Read each passage. Then circle the letter of the answer to each question.

The pile of cashmere sweaters fell over as Jacinta brushed past the front table. She was halfway across the room before she looked back and saw them lying there in a sad heap. Jacinta let out an audible sigh, put down the box of glass jars she was carrying, and grudgingly turned toward the pile of sweaters she would need to refold. She was fantasizing about what it would be like to finally quit this awful job when she tripped over the box she had left on the ground. Gently shaking the box, Jacinta heard the tinkling sound she feared.

23. What is one character trait that Jacinta shows?

  A laziness

  B clumsiness

  C gracefulness

  D focus

24. What do you predict Jacinta will find when she opens the box?

  F The glass jars will be broken.

  G The glass jars will be in perfect condition.

  H The box will be full of bells.

  J The box will be empty.

Real-life pirates are not like the pirates you see in movies or on television shows. Fictional works such as *Treasure Island* and *Peter Pan* have influenced the ways in which people think of pirates. A romantic or comical image of the pirate has developed over time, with characters often acting cheerful and lighthearted. Many fictional pirates live by a code of honor and rarely hurt anyone, while in reality, modern-day pirates often show no mercy to those who oppose them. They will attack merchant ships, fishing boats, and even cruise ships. Pirates will also turn on one another, leaving fellow pirates marooned. Many modern pirates have died from diseases and from wounds received during their voyages.

25. What is the writer comparing and contrasting in this passage?

A pirates and sailors

B fictional pirates and real-life pirates

C *Treasure Island* and *Peter Pan*

D piracy in the past and piracy in the present

26. What generalization can you make about real-life pirates?

F They are more like merchants than fictional pirates.

G They often die of scurvy.

H They are often violent.

J They are romantic and cheerful.

While biking is good exercise as well as a great way to get around without hurting the environment, many bicyclists on the roads today are endangering themselves and others. Some roadways do not have a bike lane, but even when there is one, bikers often veer in and out of it. Many cyclists don't wear helmets, or they listen to music through headphones while biking. Worst of all, many cyclists continue straight through red lights without stopping, causing drivers to brake hard or swerve.

27. Which statement supports the opinion that many bicyclists are endangering themselves and others?

A Biking is a great way to get around without hurting the environment.

B Biking is good exercise.

C Many cyclists continue straight through red lights without stopping.

D There is often no bike lane.

28. What is the best summary of this passage?

F Bicyclists often bike through red lights. There should be a law passed restricting the use of bicycles on busy streets.

G Bicycles are a great way to get around without polluting.

H While biking is good exercise and is a good way to help protect the environment, many cyclists are endangering themselves and others with their unsafe behaviors.

J Cyclists are generally unsafe and reckless people. Roadways are not meant to accommodate bikers.

Posttest continued

Read the workplace document from a policy manual. Then circle the letter of the answer to each question.

> Long Haul Enterprises wants to ensure that our drivers are rested and fit for driving whenever they are on the road. Drivers' on-duty time is limited, which will help keep drivers awake, alert, and safe. In addition to time spent driving, on-duty time is defined as including any of the following activities:
>
> - time spent inspecting, maintaining, fueling, or washing your truck
> - time spent loading or unloading your truck; time spent supervising the loading or unloading of your truck as well as associated paperwork
> - time spent taking required drug/alcohol testing as well as travel to and from the testing site
> - time spent doing any other paid work for your employer, including training

29. What effect does the company hope limited on-duty time will have?

   A help drivers pass drug/alcohol tests

   B keep drivers from taking other part-time jobs

   C keep drivers alert and safe

   D allow time to maintain vehicles

30. What is the author's purpose for creating this document?

   F to encourage drivers to work beyond their regular shift

   G to explain what activities count as on-duty time

   H to convince the government to lengthen allowable driving hours

   J to explain how truck maintenance should be scheduled

31. Based on the document, you can conclude that drivers should spend their off-duty time

   A maintaining their trucks

   B resting and sleeping

   C working at other jobs

   D doing anything they want

32. What is the main idea of the first paragraph of the document?

   F Long Haul Enterprises limits on-duty time so drivers can stay safe.

   G Long Haul Enterprise wants drivers to be fit and rested in order to maintain their trucks.

   H Long Haul Enterprise wants its drivers to drive as much as possible before they feel tired.

   J Staying awake and alert is the responsibility of every driver.

Posttest continued

Read the workplace document on hygiene procedures. Then circle the letter of the answer to each question.

> Washing hands frequently is the quickest and easiest way to prevent the spread of illnesses and infections. However, the number of people who do not know the correct procedure for this common task is surprising. As a health-care worker, it is your responsibility to remember these steps and pass them along to patients, friends, and family.
>
> First, wet hands with clean water and apply soap. Next, rub hands together for 20 seconds or more. Do not forget the backs of hands, under the fingernails, and between the fingers, as germs can hide in these spots. Finally, rinse your hands and either air dry them or use a clean towel.
>
> If you follow these steps, the use of hand sanitizer is unnecessary. If, however, you find yourself in a situation in which soap and water are not available, then an alcohol-based hand sanitizer is an acceptable substitute. Be sure to cover all parts of your hands with sanitizer and rub them together for 30 seconds. Be aware, however, that sanitizers do not eliminate all types of germs and are not effective on visibly dirty hands.

33. What is one way in which washing hands with soap and water and using hand sanitizer are different?

- **A** Hand sanitizer kills all germs, while soap and water kill only some germs.
- **B** They are exactly the same.
- **C** Hand sanitizer will not work on visibly dirty hands, but soap and water will work.
- **D** You must wash the backs of hands with soap and water, but you only need to wash the palms and fingers with hand sanitizer.

34. Which sentence is an opinion?

- **F** The number of people who do not know the correct procedure for this common task is surprising.
- **G** Rub hands together for 20 seconds or more.
- **H** Sanitizers do not eliminate all kinds of germs.
- **J** Germs can hide in these spots.

35. What effect does the writer create in this document?

- **A** loving
- **B** suspicious
- **C** angry
- **D** helpful

36. What do you predict will happen if you do not wash the backs of your hands?

- **F** Hand sanitizer will not work.
- **G** There will still be germs on your hands.
- **H** The hand washing will still be effective.
- **J** Your hands will not be visibly dirty.

37. When washing your hands with soap and water, what should you do after rubbing your hands together for 20 seconds?

- **A** apply hand sanitizer
- **B** rinse your hands for 30 seconds
- **C** rinse and dry your hands
- **D** let your hands air dry

196   Reading Basics · Advanced

Posttest continued

Circle the letter of the answer to each question.

38. Which phrase means "the ships that belong to the navy"?

   F the navys' ships

   G the navy's ships

   H the navys ship's

   J the navie's ships

39. Which word fits into both sentences?

Kimi _____ a picture of the landscape.

Thina _____ a card from the deck when it was her turn.

   A painted

   B snapped

   C drew

   D sketched

40. Which word means "having seriously damaging results"?

   F disasterious

   G disasterioin

   H disastrous

   J disasterition

41. Which word means "somewhat precious"?

   A multiprecious

   B semiprecious

   C midprecious

   D misprecious

42. What is the meaning of the word *maniacal*?

   F having the characteristics of a maniac

   G a person who is a maniac

   H partly maniac

   J more maniac

43. Which word does NOT belong in the word family?

   A scripted

   B description

   C unscripted

   D scruples

44. Which word contains the same sound as the underlined spelling in the word *laughter*?

   F popular

   G trophy

   H together

   J chapter

45. Which word completes the analogy?

Page : *book* as *note* : _____.

   A piano

   B song

   C sing

   D orchestra

46. What is the meaning of the word *triathlon*?

   F in the middle of an athletic event

   G an athletic competition that has three parts

   H among an athletic event

   J to redo an athletic event

47. What is the plural of the word *tray*?

   A trace

   B traies

   C trays

   D trayes

48. Which word means "like a fool"?

   F fooling

   G fooled

   H foolish

   J semifool

49. Which word is an antonym of the underlined word?

idle person

   A busy

   B lazy

   C overweight

   D tired

50. Which word means "more shiny"?

- **F** shinyer
- **G** shinyier
- **H** shinier
- **J** shinyiest

51. Which two words are homophones?

- **A** fort, fount
- **B** forth, fourth
- **C** first, fierce
- **D** fancy, fence

52. Which word is the correct contraction of *I will*?

- **F** I'ill
- **G** I'll
- **H** Ill'
- **J** I'will

53. Which word is a synonym of the underlined word?
<u>expensive</u> dinner

- **A** cheap
- **B** high-priced
- **C** delicious
- **D** overcooked

54. Which word is the plural of the word *mess*?

- **F** messes
- **G** messed
- **H** messies
- **J** messches

55. Which word means "the state of being soft"?

- **A** softship
- **B** softive
- **C** softness
- **D** softious

56. Which word has the Latin root meaning "carry"?

- **F** contradict
- **G** transport
- **H** inscribe
- **J** erupt

57. Which word means the opposite of the underlined word?
<u>orderly</u> library

- **A** organized
- **B** chaotic
- **C** tall
- **D** empty

58. Which word fits into both sentences?
The song was a number one _____.
Casey _____ the ball over the fence.

- **F** threw
- **G** hit
- **H** seller
- **J** saw

59. Which word means "of two coasts"?

- **A** unicoastal
- **B** tricoastal
- **C** bicoastal
- **D** semicoastal

60. Which word means "not acceptable"?

- **F** misacceptable
- **G** nonacceptable
- **H** unacceptable
- **J** disacceptable

61. Which word means "between states"?

- **A** interstate
- **B** superstate
- **C** semistate
- **D** unistate

62. Which word is a synonym for the underlined word?
<u>tough</u> leather

- **F** soft
- **G** cracked
- **H** sturdy
- **J** brown

POSTTEST EVALUATION CHART AND ANSWER KEY

This posttest was designed to check your mastery of the reading skills studied. Use the key on page 200. Then circle the question numbers that you answered incorrectly and review the practice pages covering those skills. Carefully rework those practice pages to be sure you understand those skills.

Tested Skills	Question Numbers	Practice Pages
Recognize and Recall Details	9, 15, 17	14–17
Stated and Implied Concepts	4, 12	22–25
Draw Conclusions	2, 20, 31	30–33
Summarize and Paraphrase	5, 28	38–41
Identify Cause and Effect	1, 29	46–49
Understand Author's Purpose	7, 30	54–57
Find the Main Idea	3, 32	62–65
Identify Sequence	16, 19, 37	78–81
Understand Consumer Materials	21, 22	86–89
Use Reference Sources/Maps	8	94–97
Use Supporting Evidence	27	102–105
Recognize Character Traits	23	110–113
Identify Style Techniques	11	118–121
Make Generalizations	26	134–137
Author's Effect and Intention	13, 35	142–145
Compare and Contrast	25, 33	150–153
Predict Outcomes	24, 36	158–161
Identify Fact and Opinion	6, 34	166–169
Identify Genre	14	174–177
Spelling	38, 47, 51, 52, 54	20, 28, 44, 45, 52, 60, 108, 157, 181
Synonyms/Antonyms	49, 53, 57, 62	37, 124, 140, 148
Context Clues	10, 18, 39, 58	21, 53, 69, 85, 101, 117, 173
Word Analysis	40–46, 48, 50, 55, 56, 59, 60, 61	20, 29, 36, 44, 52, 60, 61, 68, 84, 92, 93, 100, 108, 109, 116, 124, 125, 140, 141, 148, 149, 156, 164, 165, 172, 180

KEY			
1.	A	32.	F
2.	F	33.	C
3.	A	34.	F
4.	J	35.	D
5.	B	36.	G
6.	J	37.	C
7.	A	38.	G
8.	F	39.	C
9.	A	40.	H
10.	F	41.	B
11.	C	42.	F
12.	J	43.	D
13.	D	44.	G
14.	F	45.	B
15.	B	46.	G
16.	H	47.	C
17.	D	48.	H
18.	F	49.	A
19.	C	50.	H
20.	F	51.	B
21.	C	52.	G
22.	J	53.	B
23.	B	54.	F
24.	F	55.	C
25.	B	56.	G
26.	H	57.	B
27.	C	58.	G
28.	H	59.	C
29.	C	60.	H
30.	G	61.	A
31.	B	62.	H